The Flying Bomb War

By the same author:

The Day War Broke Out
Spitfire Summer

THE FLYING BOMB WAR

Contemporary Eyewitness
Accounts of the German V-1
and V-2 Raids on Britain

PETER HAINING

ROBSON BOOKS

First published in Great Britain in 2002 by Robson Books, 64 Brewery Road, London, N7 9NT

A member of **Chrysalis** Books plc

British Library Cataloguing in Publication Data
A catalogue record for this title is available from the British Library.

ISBN 1 86105 581 1

Picture credits
Pictures from author's personal collection.

Typeset by FiSH Books, London WC1
Printed by Mackays of Chatham, Kent

This book is for my mother
who lived through
The Flying Bomb War

Contents

Contents

Prelude

'It started out like any other Saturday morning. I was walking along the High Road in Tottenham with my two kids going to my mum's as I usually did, when I heard this flying bomb go overhead. It was making an awful noise. I hid with the children until I heard the sound of it exploding.

'After a bit we all ran down the road to where my mother lived just in case the bomb had landed anywhere near her house. I was ever so relieved to find that it hadn't and she was perfectly all right. In fact, I didn't think anything more about it until I went home in the afternoon.

'When I reached my street I just couldn't believe what I saw. There was debris and rubble everywhere. It had been *my* house that the flying bomb had hit!'

Mrs Lil Charles, now of Harlow New Town,
talking to the author about the V-1
she witnessed on 17 June 1944.

Introduction
Genesis of the V-Weapons

Sixty years ago, on 3 October 1942, the prototype German V-2 rocket – which was also the world's first practical liquid-fuel rocket – was successfully launched from a secret base at Peenemünde on the Baltic Island of Usedom... and the Space Age was born. Just over two months later, on Christmas Eve, a second prototype, the V-1, the first pilotless, weapon-carrying aircraft, was also fired from the same site... and the era of the 'Doodlebug' began. Together these two unique and deadly ballistic missiles were destined to attack England in a merciless and bloody onslaught that has since become known as 'The Flying Bomb War'.

Although Germany and the Allied Forces were at that time already locked in the massive confrontation of the Second World War which would ultimately bring down Adolf Hitler's much-vaunted 'Thousand Year Reich', the 120-mile, controlled flight of the bullet-shaped V-2 which reached a height of 50 miles and a speed of 3,300 miles per hour, was to provide the breakthrough in making possible mankind's long held dream of conquering space. And to lead, in the fullness of time, to the Sputnik era, men on the moon, and the most recent plans to put astronauts onto the planet Mars. Similarly, the successful flight of the V-1 was the realisation of the idea of remote-controlled jet aircraft that had challenged experimenters in Europe and America for almost half a century.

3

Today at Peenemünde, where these dreams became realities, there is a small museum and, in a closed military security area, the test site, or *Prufstande*, surrounded by high fencing and banned to the public. It appears inhabited only by the ghosts of some of the 5,000 people who built the weapons of mass destruction that became the means of reaching the stars. Everywhere lie skeletons of tangled steel girders and piles of shattered concrete, the last remnants of the German rocket wizardry that nearly, very nearly, tipped the balance of the war.

Amidst the clusters of trees and tangle of vegetation there are to be found the remains of Test-Pad No. 7, a large basin now full of water and enclosed by stumps of reinforced concrete, from which that first V-2 was launched. Not far away are the remnants of a 'ski-ramp' that launched the prototype V-1s across the Baltic Sea. Still visible, too, is the shell of the liquid-oxygen plant that once manufactured the fuel for the rockets, and the collapsed panels of some supersonic wind tunnels – the first of their kind in the world. Between all these remains, rusting and weed-covered, run miles of railway lines which half a century ago linked the site to the vast network of underground tunnels and bunkers.

Peenemünde has, in truth, always been a bleak spot. It lies on the extreme north-western tip of Usedom facing the narrow neck of sea that broadens as it runs down the coast to the city of Stettin, once part of East Germany until the reunification. The site did not, in fact, fall into the hands of the Allies until the end of the war, at which time the German physicists who had worked there were eagerly 'recruited' by the Americans and Russians to form the nucleus of their embryo teams of space scientists. After that, the site was reduced to rubble.

But memories of the V-1 and V-2 have never dimmed: neither here along the Baltic coast nor, more particularly, in England where their devastating impact was felt by hundreds of thousands of people who became the targets of the two waves of Hitler's *Vergeltungswaffe* or 'Revenge Weapons'.

In Britain both these missiles have a permanent place in the public consciousness – and not just among those people still alive to tell the tale of their coming. At a number of churches in Kent and Sussex, for instance, there are graves and memorial plaques to be seen recording the deaths of victims of the weapons, while in a number of the further-flung counties such as Essex and Suffolk the physical scars of their attacks can be found in the form of water-filled craters. At the Science Museum and Imperial War Museum in London perfect specimens of both weapons are on display, attracting large crowds of all ages; and it is by no means uncommon to find them evocatively used in newspaper headlines: *vide* the one which appeared as recently as 3 December 1989 in the *Sunday Express* asking: 'Will Doodlebug Pound Push Up Interest Rates?'

Along the German coast from Stettin to Kolberg it is still possible to find elderly residents who remember the tremendous roar of the rockets when they were first being launched from the island. Some talk particularly of the strange 'frozen lightning' that was seen high in the sky when the number of tests multiplied. But what none of these people knew then was the real purpose and destination of the rockets – though the indications were unavoidable after one terrible night in 1943 when a large force of British bombers flew overhead, bombed Peenemünde, and killed over 2,200 people: scientists, technicians and workers.

It was not, in fact, until June 1990, forty-five years after the Russians had razed the site to the ground, that the first journalists were allowed back onto the island. In a tour carefully orchestrated by the Communist authorities, a dozen reporters from the leading Western news organisations were shown over the gaunt ruins of the wizard's den where the deadly flying weapons had been developed. The party was led by a Captain Bernd Fischer of the East German Navy who explained to his guests how the weapons had been developed under the command of Major General Walter Dornberger – the man responsible for the creation of the site – and through the genius of a young scientist named Wernher von Braun, who was later to play such a leading role in the American space programme.

'You are now standing where space history began in October 1942,' Captain Fischer told his party, indicating the desolate, ruined landscape. 'From here, for the first time in history, a machine built by man was launched into the atmosphere and returned to hit the Earth with a force equivalent to that of fifty one-hundred-ton express locomotives travelling at sixty miles per hour.'

If the Captain's words sounded a little grandiose to his layman audience, the facts which have come to light in the intervening years since that first flight of the V-2 more than justify the claim.

It was, in fact, just over a year after the British bombing raid on Peenemünde – on 8 September 1944 – that the first of the V-2s developed on the island fell like the clap of doom onto the people of south-east England. A people who were then just congratulating themselves on having withstood the fury of the rocket's predecessor, the V-1 or 'Doodlebug' as it had become popularly known – the first of which had roared across the English coast to plunge on an unsuspecting target earlier that same summer.

Though far fewer of the much deadlier V-2s were to be launched against Britain during the war of the flying bombs, they were to take an equally terrible toll of human life and property – as the statistics reveal. Though figures can never convey the real cost in terms of human suffering and misery, they still make chilling reading today.

The records indicate that a total of 10,492 V-1s were launched by the Germans between June 1944 and March 1945, of which 3,957 were destroyed by British defences (the artillery batteries and RAF fighter pilots). But those that got through and struck their targets were responsible for killing 6,184 people and seriously injuring another 17,981.

By contrast, just 1,115 of the huge V-2s were aimed at southern England – London in particular – in the months from September 1944 to March 1945, and although quite a high percentage blew up on the way, they still killed 2,855 people and seriously hurt 6,268.

These terrible statistics are, in fact, part of the price man has paid for conquering space. For London was the unwitting testing ground for the forerunners of the rockets that later journeyed into space with such amazing precision. As one East Ender reminded me while I was compiling this book: Bethnal Green may well be 4,500 miles from Cape Canaveral but both share a common connection through the V-2. It was, in fact, a direct forerunner of the rocket that enabled Neil Armstrong to be the first man on the moon in July 1969 which had fallen on a block of flats in Bethnal Green a quarter of a century earlier killing 130 people, he told me with more than a hint of emotion in his voice.

Indeed, those words are still fixed in my mind today as a grim reminder of the unmentioned, almost unmentionable, cost of space travel.

Although the rocket technology displayed by the German scientists in creating the V-1 and V-2 was undoubtedly brilliant and (as time has subsequently shown) potentially boundless in its application, it was certainly not *new*. Men had been making rockets for centuries and for at least several generations had perceived their use for travel through space. Even the idea of remotely controlled pilotless aircraft carrying warheads belonged to the years of the First World War.

The rocket is, in fact, one of the oldest forms of automation, pre-dating the steam-engine, the automobile and the aircraft by some centuries. The Chinese are generally credited with having discovered gunpowder, and by compacting it into a hollow stick they produced the first rockets. The application of this device as an implement of warfare is believed to have been first used by the Mongol hordes who passed it on to the Arabs. They, in turn, provided Europeans with their first taste of the rocket's power: using it to slaughter troops and win battles. But the Europeans were not slow in learning the lesson – or in obtaining the secret of making gunpowder for their own use.

By the Renaissance, rockets were known all over the civilised world, but although their value as a weapon was appreciated they were still not fully understood. It was that brilliant scientist Isaac Newton who enunciated the three basic laws of mechanics that so aptly describe the motion of a rocket.

In the early years of the nineteenth century a British officer named William Congreve was responsible for the next major development in rocketry – modifying one so that it could be used as a missile for bombardment. The genius of Congreve's design was spectacularly demonstrated when the Royal Navy used some 40,000 rockets in the destruction of Copenhagen. By the Napoleonic era, all the major armies of Europe had introduced rocket corps into their front-line troops and for a time it seemed that no campaign was likely to succeed without the support of these implements raining death from the skies.

The rocket was still, though, a basically inaccurate weapon and this finally led the Army to abandon it in favour of the precision aim of the rifle. Although it remained popular as a means of providing spectacular entertainment in the form of the skyrocket, the limitations of the gunpowder with its single explosion restricted any further real development. A more controllable fuel, probably in liquid form, which could be converted into gas and released in a series of explosions to propel the rocket forward continuously was what was required.

The first man to propose such a 'pulse-jet', as it became known, was a Frenchman named Victor de Karavodine in the year 1906. Although little is known of the man himself, the patent he lodged in Paris on 6 April 1906, number 374,124, still exists and shows the details of a pulse-jet which would use a low-pressure supercharger to pump fuel into a combustion chamber and a sparking plug to ignite it. Four years later, a Belgian, George Marconnet, also took plans for a jet-propulsion system to the Paris patent office and registered them on 10 February 1910 as patent number 412,478. Although Marconnet, who was a commercial engineer by profession, did not take de Karavodine's idea a great deal further, he did prophetically predict that it would be 'particularly suitable for aeroplanes and airships'. Looking at his plans today, it is possible to see in them some remarkable similarities to the propulsion unit developed by the Germans for the V-1.

The first plan for a pilotless missile carrying a warhead was the idea of another Frenchman, René Lorin, an artillery officer, who claimed to have been working on the idea since 1907, although he did not actually publish the details until 1919 in a short book entitled *L'Air et la Vitesse*. In this he described how an unmanned aircraft, propelled by a pulse-jet and stabilised by gyroscopes, could be guided to its target by radio control from another aircraft which would stay out of range of enemy defences. Lorin, who was evidently something of a patriot, claimed his machine could carry a 440lb warhead, and launched from Paris would have no difficulty in reaching Berlin and dropping its explosives. However, the fact that the Armistice with Germany had already been signed probably ended what little official interest there might have been in the Frenchman's idea!

What is certainly true is that neither Lorin's engine – nor those of his predecessors, for that matter – were ever built. Nevertheless, what he in particular had conceived was to prove virtually the prototype of the unmanned missile which a decade later would fly against England when the dark clouds of war had once again gathered over the same European nations.

The three men, de Karavodine, Marconnet and Lorin, were, of course, all theorists. Robert H Goddard, an American inventor who followed in their stead, was a practical experimenter, and he it was who first developed the fuel necessary for their rockets to fly: a mixture of petrol and liquid oxygen. In 1919 he published a ground-breaking paper, 'A Method of Reaching Extreme Altitudes', in which he stated that the rocket did not have to be large or heavy 'provided the gases of the jet were ejected from the rocket at high velocity, and also provided that most of the rocket consisted of propellant material'. Goddard, it should be stressed, saw his rockets very much as a means of space travel and not of mass destruction.

Following several years of intensive research, Goddard launched the world's first liquid-fuelled rocket on 16 March 1926. The tiny projectile flew erratically for only 2.5 seconds and barely exceeded 60 m.p.h. – but the principle of liquid-fuel jet propulsion had been proven. In the succeeding years he made several hundred more rocket firings, his projectiles hurtling up to ever-increasing altitudes, and it is true to say that in his work he experimented with almost every component of modern rocketry.

What, however, remains a curious fact is that very little attention was paid in America to Goddard's work, although his experiments were being studied with increasing interest by a number of experimenters in Germany who had similarly come to appreciate the potential of liquid-fuel rockets; in particular, by a group based in Berlin known as The Society for Space Flight, founded by a Transylvanian Saxon named Herman Oberth and numbering among its most enthusiastic members a young man named Wernher von Braun. As early as 1923, Oberth had been suggesting that liquid-fuel rockets would provide the means for making interplanetary flights, and he and the other members conducted a number of successful launches with small rocket motors during the ensuing years.

In 1929 Oberth published a book about these experiments, *The Way To Space*, that might well have earned the Society Government backing if it had not become riven by internal disputes, brought about by the political climate in Germany, and resulting in its dissolution. One group who showed particular interest in the experiments was the emerging Nazi Party, and even before the members had gone their separate ways, the Gestapo had moved into their clubhouse and seized all the files.

These documents and plans, as well as a number of the youthful experimenters, were destined to be brought together again a little later when the leader of the Nazi Party was made aware of the awesome potential of such rockets for destruction – and, more specifically, revenge...

Throughout the early Thirties the ideas of jet-propulsion and pilotless aircraft continued to interest aeronautical experimenters on both sides of the Atlantic. The Americans, for instance, flew 'The Bug', a pilotless, bomb-carrying aircraft that was powered by a conventional engine but was restricted by its very limited range; while the British successfully launched a number of 'Queen Bees', a radio-controlled plane not unlike the famous Tiger Moth which was used for target practice but had a frame which was too light and an engine with insufficient power to carry offensive weapons.

In Germany, however, the idea for a pulse-jet proposed by René Lorin continued to absorb the mind of a brilliant inventor named Dr Paul Schmidt and led to him developing a 'duct' engine which he claimed could be used to propel a 'flying torpedo'. At the same time, and quite independently, another aircraft engine design team at the Argus Motorenwerke factory under the direction of a technical wizard called Dr Fritz Gosslau produced the Argus Duct which was similar in construction and purpose. However, when these two engines were demonstrated to high-ranking officers of the German Army and the Luftwaffe, the consensus of opinion was that it would be hard to find a practical use for them unless their short operational life could be improved and their range much extended.

The man who was responsible for changing the minds of these military and air force officers about the potential of jet power was an artilleryman, Captain Walter Dornberger, who for some time had been nursing an instinct about the potential of rocket weapons. Dornberger had been seconded to the Ballistics and Munitions Section of the German Army Weapons Office, and there started to develop long-range rockets driven by liquid fuel along similar lines to those proposed by Herman Oberth. To assist him in this work, he recruited Wernher von Braun, then still only in his early twenties, and by 1936 the two men had created the basic design for the large rocket that would ultimately become the V-2.

The persuasive Dornberger also managed to talk the Luftwaffe into sharing costs with the German War Office in the opening up of a secret testing station for the rockets. The site chosen was the remote island of Usedom, ideally placed 70 miles from the nearest city and surrounded by 300 miles of open sea which could be used for a firing range. At a cost of 300 million marks and under a cloak of tightly controlled security, the vast laboratories and testing grounds of Peenemünde were constructed.

By the autumn of 1939, when Hitler had plunged Germany into war with Britain, the research of Dornberger and von Braun had progressed far enough for the Führer to be given a demonstration of one of their rocket propulsion units. Hitler, however, was singularly unimpressed: he preferred, he told his officers, to put his faith in massive conventional forces to bring the British to their knees.

At much this same time, a new proposal from Argus Motorenwerke for a remotely controlled pilotless aircraft with a range of 350 miles, propelled by either a piston-engine, turbo-jet or ducted fan for use in reconnaissance, was also demonstrated and similarly greeted with a lack of enthusiasm by the German Air Ministry.

But this indifference changed dramatically after one traumatic night in the spring of 1942. Indeed, it is probably true to say that the course of the war was changed when British Bomber Command carried out a new style of incendiary bombing on the ancient German town of Lübeck. In just a few hours on 28 March over 200 acres of buildings were destroyed by a cascade of fire bombs. On hearing of this destruction, an enraged Hitler ordered that 'attacks of a retaliatory nature' were to be made on British non-military targets – and to carry out his wishes he gave instructions for a force of *Vergeltungswaffe*, or 'Revenge Weapons', to be created. First, though, the weapons had to be developed.

One immediate possibility was found at Peenemünde where Wernher von Braun had now become the world's leading authority on rocket propulsion. He and his team were on the verge of making their first trial launchings of a ballistic missile they called the A-4, a rocket which had been painstakingly developed from three earlier prototypes. (The A, incidentally, signified the German word *Aggregat* meaning assembly.) The rocket was a breathtaking sight: 46 feet high with a motor so large a man could crawl through the nozzle, it had been estimated that after launching it would reach a speed of over 3,000 miles per hour in just 65 seconds! And when the A-4 was fired on 3 October of that same year, those present knew they had developed one of the weapons that Hitler was seeking.

The Luftwaffe was also anxious to make its own contribution to the Führer's call, and when Fritz Gosslau of Argus Motorenwerke put forward another plan for a more sophisticated pilotless bombardment aircraft powered by a pulse jet his timing could not have been better. The man to whom he showed his designs was Field Marshal Erhard Milch, the Inspector-General of the German Air Force and deputy to Reichsmarschall Hermann Goering. Milch was immediately attracted to the idea and swept aside all objections: the development of the Fiesler 103 – a cover-name based on the manufacturing company, Fieseler Flugzeugbau – was given the highest priority and by late November trials of unpowered prototypes were being conducted at Peenemünde.

Then on 24 December 1942, just over two months after the first V-2 had been launched from Peenemünde, the Fieseler 103 was fired from a catapult ramp on the same site and sped away across the turbulent green waters of the Baltic. Vengeance Weapon 1, the 'Flying Bomb', was now also more than just a designer's dream.

In July 1943, film of the launching of an A-4 at Peenemünde was shown to Hitler. By all accounts the Führer sat back in his chair absolutely stunned, his previous scepticism swept away as he watched the mighty ballistic missile speed up into the sky. And when an equally impressive report on the Fi.103, prepared by the Long-Range Bombardment Commission, was handed to the German leader, he gave immediate orders for work to go ahead on both 'Revenge Weapons' 'with the highest priority'.

This is perhaps a suitable juncture at which to give a little more technical information about these two aerial weapons which were to wreak such death and destruction on the British population. It is, though, important to remember that it was to be some while before the British Government knew all the details about them, and even longer before the general public were given the facts about what was blasting from the skies into their daily lives.

It was, in all probability, the remarkable speed with which the V-1 was transformed from a drawing-board concept into an operable weapon – plus the fact it could be manufactured in fewer man-hours (about 50), cost a great deal less than the huge V-2 (about £150 each), and flew on low grade fuel – which first brought it into action against England. The pilotless missile was 25 feet long, made of steel, and had a wing span of just over 17 feet with a single fin and rudder at the rear. At the time of launching, it weighed about two tons, including half a ton of fuel and an explosive charge of just under a ton. This warhead consisted of TNT – the explosive most commonly used by both sides during the war – and was exploded by two impact fuses. The pulse-jet power

14

unit consisted of an Argus duct modified by the incorporation of the valve-system of the Schmidt duct, and its supply of fuel was sufficient for it to remain in the air for between thirty minutes and an hour. Initially, the V-1 had a range of about 160 miles, but this was later increased to 250 when the advancing Allied Forces pushed the Germans back out of northern France, and the missiles had to be launched from Holland. The V-1 flew at an altitude of between two and three thousand feet – then the most awkward height for anti-aircraft fire – at an average speed of 370 m.p.h., with 400 m.p.h. the maximum obtainable.

Although rocket engineers had long believed that such a 'flying torpedo' would have to be radio-controlled (and, indeed, when the first V-1s descended on England, the newspaper reports stated that they were), the rocket actually had a pre-set automatic guidance system. Launched in the direction of its target, the flight of the aircraft was controlled by a magnetic compass, two gyroscopes incorporating an accelerometer (a type of speedometer that sensed deviations and sent correcting signals to the control surface actuators), a barometer to gauge altitude, and a small propeller on the nose to measure the distance travelled. This propeller was pre-set to trip a switch arming the warhead when the V-1 was 35 miles from its target, and when this was reached a tachometer switched on an electromechanical device which cancelled the gyroscopes and caused the weapon to swing into an uncertain dive.

I say uncertain because, once the gyroscopic controls had been cancelled, any inequality in weight between the wings immediately swung the machine slightly off course as it dived. And, similarly, the shut-off of the engine caused by depriving it of fuel prevented the power-dive its creators had sought in order to achieve a deeper penetration into the ground and thereby a more effective explosion.

The noise the V-1 made was never forgotten by anyone who heard it. 'A grating, sinister growl which increased as it approached to a most menacing roar', according to one

15

acoustically attuned eyewitness, while two more mechanically minded observers compared it to 'a Model-T Ford going up a hill', or 'a disagreeable splutter, like an aerial motorcycle in bad running order'. In fact, the sound was generated by the way in which the missile functioned after air had been drawn into the combustion chamber through its series of spring-loaded, non-return flapper valves. These valves, when they closed, allowed the fuel from the gas-pressurised tank to be sprayed in and ignited. The resultant gas then jetted from the exhaust with a thrust of 575lb, forcing the V-1 forward. The flapper valves again opened and the process would be repeated – with the cycle occurring so rapidly that the residual fire from one explosion ignited the next.

The normal method of launching the missile was from a tilted ramp referred to as a 'ski site' in British reports – by means of an explosive device which made use of the powerful reaction between hydrogen peroxide and permanganate of potash. Alternatively, it could be launched from a specially modified Heinkel 111 aircraft, but fewer than a fifth of the total V-1s targeted on England ever were – and those mostly towards the end of the campaign as the Germans were pushed back ever closer to their own borders.

No matter how the V-1 was dispatched, its arrival in England was always the same, as the author and wartime pilot H E Bates, who saw and heard many of them, has so evocatively recalled:

At the end of its journey, the bomb began to dive. Its propulsion unit petered out through lack of fuel, the monoplane became soundless, except for a strange and eerie rustling sound, and after an interval, sometimes very short, sometimes uncannily long, the bomb hit earth and exploded.

This explosion was dynamic. The effect was not downward, into the earth, so that on all occasions the crater it made was astonishingly shallow and small, but outward, in the immensity of its surface blast. Its noise could be heard at a great distance; its effect would be felt over miles. The blast struck houses and large buildings and disintegrated them like a tornado against a house of straw. A single bomb could lay a country parish in ruins. It could blast the houses of a dozen streets. It could make homeless, even if temporarily homeless, hundreds of people. It could blow the bodies of its victims into small pieces, far afield. It could not only kill but cause, in the lives of hundreds of people over its course and at its destination, terror and misery and all the disheartening nuisances of disrupted life and homelessness.

The V-2, of course, was a much bigger, costlier and potentially deadlier weapon altogether. Wernher von Braun who was in a position to know such things estimated in 1943 that it cost in excess of 30,000 marks to make one and took at least ten times as many man-hours as a V-1 to build.

In technical terms, the missile was a single-stage, gyroscopically stabilised, finned rocket, 46 feet long, with a diameter around the middle of five and a half feet. It was armed with a one-ton warhead containing 1,650lb of explosives, and this, plus roughly four tons of fuel, consisting of a three-to-one mixture of ethyl alcohol and water and about five tons of liquid oxygen forced into the combustion chamber by powerful pumps and burned at the rate of 275lb per second, gave it a take-off weight of nearly 13 tons! Perhaps it comes as no surprise to learn that the missile seemed to take off with agonising slowness, but once the impetus of its 25-ton initial thrust began to take effect, it reached supersonic speed in under 30 seconds.

The range of the V-2, which was launched in an upright position from a portable stand on a concrete base, was between 200 and 220 miles, and when on course for a target reached a height of 50 to 60 miles at the peak of its trajectory while travelling at 3,500 m.p.h. Despite being slowed by its re-entry into the earth's atmosphere, the lethal combination of steel and explosives would still be travelling at around 2,500 m.p.h. at the moment of impact.

The control and stability of the rocket was achieved by the gyroscopic system which was linked to a set of vanes at the rear of its fins, as well as a secondary set positioned in the exhaust. The usual method of controlling the direction was to pre-set the system so that it held the rocket on a calculated line by trimming the vanes to correct any deviations. Alternatively, the missile could be controlled by a pre-set 'accelometer' which turned off the fuel when it had attained a given speed; or by a radio beam – but this was only possible where the beam-transmitter could be sited in exactly the right relationship to the rocket and its launching point.

The V-2 had two major advantages over the V-1. Firstly, because it flew in a giant arc and not on a straight line, it was invulnerable to attack by guns or aircraft. And, secondly, because it flew faster than sound it gave no warning of its approach until the terrible moment when it struck. Indeed, only in the last few seconds was it ever visible to the naked eye, and then only really at night as a dull-red meteorlike object heated to incandescence by atmospheric friction. Equally true is the fact that no one – neither a pilot nor a land-based artilleryman – ever attempted to shoot down a V-2: indeed it would have been quite futile to try.

But the rocket did have its disadvantages, too, for not only did each one take a long time to manufacture, but it used up vast quantities of top grade fuel and could be very unstable on launching. The numbers of V-2s that blew up while preparing for take-off or soon afterwards is believed to have exceeded a hundred – with consequent loss of German personnel and valuable equipment. However, once in the air the rocket was unstoppable, irrevocably destined to hit its target, and was able to inflict terrible casualties by its explosion – facts that make it a surprise to read that according to at least one authority it was considered less frightening than its predecessor. I quote Basil Collier in his book *The Battle of the V-Weapons* (1964):

On the whole, the British public found the V-2 a less alarming weapon than the V-1. This was partly, of course, because far fewer rockets than flying bombs reached the country, but it was also partly because the rocket arrived unheralded by the dismal rattle of the bomb, and often unnoticed by people outside the immediate vicinity of the point of impact. Another factor which helped make the V-2 less disturbing to the peace of mind of the ordinary citizen was that damage done by the rocket was confined, as a rule, to a comparatively small area.

There were undoubtedly, though, many folk who found themselves in the vicinity of an explosion caused by one of these bolts from the blue – and lived to tell the tale – who certainly did *not* share this opinion. Indeed, my own researches suggest that a great many men and women living in the centre of London who experienced the attacks were left in no doubt that the V-2 was the most awesome weapon ever launched against this country by Hitler. If their awe has been in any way affected by the passage of time it has been quite simply by the development of those same V-2s into space rockets.

It was during the first few days of 1943, just after the people of the beleaguered British Isles had made the best of their fourth Christmas of the war, that Intelligence sources in London received their first reports from Allied agents that the Germans were testing secret rocket weapons at Peenemünde.

There were initial fears that these stories of 'Science Fiction' weapons being made for use in the war were just a cleverly contrived Nazi hoax. But when aerial reconnaissance by British planes brought back clear proof of several unexplained structures on Usedom, the War Cabinet decided to set up a special investigative committee under the leadership of Mr Duncan Sandys, a former Parliamentary Secretary

THE FLYING BOMB WAR

in the Ministry of Supply and the son-in-law of the Prime Minister, Winston Churchill. With typical British archaic humour, the committee was codenamed 'Crossbow'.

Duncan Sandys, an experienced artillery officer and a man familiar with such rocket development as had been carried out in Britain, approached his task with a commendably open mind, and by the late spring of 1943 was convinced that there were not one but two types of weapon being developed at Peenemünde. The photographs of the site which returning aircraft brought home revealed quite clearly several tall, columnar objects about 40 feet long which were judged to be large rockets probably capable of carrying several tons of explosives. But there was also something else on what seemed to be a ramp-like structure pointing out to sea.

It was a young WAAF officer, Constance Babington Smith, working in the Central Interpretation Unit, who became the first person on the Allied side to spot a V-1 on its 'ski site'. This little moment of rocket history occurred while she was poring over yet another batch of recon-naissance shots which had been taken at the base on 23 June. What she saw and later reported to her superiors – thereby confirming as fact what had previously been only guess-work – she later described in an interview, which is given here because of its singular importance in our story.

'Presumably because of my previous interest in aviation, in 1939 I was commissioned in the WAAF and was posted to a Photographic Interpretation Unit,' Miss Babington Smith said. 'My job was to examine air photographs taken from reconnaissance aircraft – not too easy, as the camera would be about 30,000 feet above its subject. Yet it was fascinating work, giving a real thrill with every success.

'In May 1943, I was at Medmenham, not far from Henley. My laboratory was not very prepossessing – in fact, it was just a bathroom. However, I used very few technical appliances, so I managed.

'I remember one day receiving a new batch of photographs.

20

I was given no hint that might lead to subconscious suggestions instead of deductive accuracy. For all I knew, the pictures might be those of a new bombing area. It was easy to identify sheds, houses and factory buildings. But one dark smudge intrigued me – a shapeless blob near the middle of the picture. I looked and looked. Finally, I thought it might be some kind of ramp.

'Then evidently another reconnaissance raid was carried out, for I got another batch of photographs for examination. There was the blob again – yes, it was a ramp. And at one end of it was a pinpoint of white.

'A little later I went to my superior officer and told him that the spot on the ramp was a small aircraft. He was rather impatient, for he couldn't make it out himself, but at last he said, "Well, if you say that it's an aeroplane, then it's an aeroplane." To me it was unmistakable – I could tell by its light and shadows. But what was an aircraft doing on a ramp? It suggested a special launching site – but that was beyond my province. The technicians took over.

'Later, I examined many other photographs in different places and identified similar ramps. Of course, at that time we had not heard the term "Flying Bomb" or V-1. We knew that the aircraft on the ramps were tailless, and the technicians suspected that the Germans had been working on tailless aircraft. So we called this new identification Peenemünde 30.'

The devastating British bomber raid on Peenemünde which followed this discovery (over 1,940 tons of bombs were dropped) took the Germans completely by surprise and it was several months before the site was operational again. As a result, the original plan for both of the V-weapons to be developed and assembled at the site had to be abandoned. It was decided to press on with testing the smaller and easier to hide V-1 there, but find another haven for the giant V-2.

During that winter, test firing of the pilotless plane

continued at Peenemünde, and by early 1944 the number of failures had dropped from 39 per cent to a remarkable 5 per cent! The actual manufacture of the V-1 along with that of the V-2 was, however, now being carried out at a vast underground factory near Nordhausen in the Harz Mountains, and from here the pilotless aircraft with their launchers were distributed all over Occupied France to be ready to begin the campaign of assault against Britain. A campaign which, in fact, when it began in June 1944 was to become a part of Germany's desperate last throw – for by then, of course, the Allied Forces had already landed in Western Normandy and begun their inexorable march towards the heart of the Nazi Reich.

Following the bombing raid on Peenemünde, the trials of the V-2 were shifted away to a more distant and better camouflaged site at Blizna in Poland. When they, too, became operational in September 1944, virtually all were launched from specially prepared sites in Holland, from the area around The Hague.

As it became ever more obvious to the British Government that these V-weapons were going to be used against the country sooner rather than later, it was decided to capitalise on all the good work Duncan Sandys had done by appointing him as chairman of a new organisation whose title was self-explanatory: The Flying Bomb Countermeasures Committee. One of its first actions was to code-name the two missiles: 'Diver' for the pilotless plane and 'Big Ben' for the rocket. The second was to begin the liaison with the forces that would have to face these new terror weapons.

Information collected by Intelligence sources soon began to pin-point where the Germans were setting up bases to launch the weapons in northern France. And from these reports it was estimated – very over-enthusiastically as it transpired – that when operational as many as 1,000 of the 'flying mines' might be launched over the Channel onto southern England *every day*! It was guessed, too – though rather more accurately – that if the large rocket was used it would probably be in clusters of from two to six with the attacks concentrated on London, then the world's most populous city.

The British and American Air Force bombers – for the USA was by now, of course, very much involved in the war – were ordered to redouble their missions against all reported sites; while plans were drawn up to defend the country through the joint efforts of the Anti-Aircraft guns and the RAF's fighter pilots.

Curiously, the involvement of American bombers in the raids on the V-1 sites, which were then understandably classified as secret, prompted some wildly improbable stories to circulate in the USA about the Nazi plans for bombarding London, as Joseph Warner Angell, a member of the USAF who was also for a time involved in the 'Crossbow' team, revealed in an article, 'Guided Missiles Could Have Won The War', published in 1952:

A few military and civilian analysts regarded the whole series of V-weapon launching sites as a gigantic hoax by the Germans, a deliberate fraud of the first magnitude designed to frighten or divert the attention and effort of the Allies from any attempts to invade the coast of France. A larger number of scientists and technicians, however, were of the opinion that the bigger sites were being prepared to launch huge rockets weighing as much as 100 tons and the smaller ramps were to send vast numbers of the Peenemünde pilotless aircraft, estimated to weigh 20 tons, against the civilians of London and against Allied troop and supply concentrations.

Rumour added other interpretations. The Germans, it was reported, were preparing to bombard London with huge containers bearing gruesome and fatal 'Red Death'; the Germans were preparing to shoot enormous tanks of poison gas to destroy every living creature in the British Isles; the Germans, even, were preparing a gigantic refrigerating apparatus along the French coast for the instantaneous creation of massive icebergs in the Channel or for dropping clouds of ice over England to stop the Allied bombers in the air.

The conflicting opinions of the experts seemed nearly irreconcilable. But clearly the Allies must do *something*. They made their decision: the V-weapon sites must be neutralised, and if possible destroyed, by aerial bombardment. It was by no means an easy decision, for withdrawing the air power to bombard the sites into uselessness might easily jeopardise the double strategy of the Allied Combined Bomber Offensive – destruction by air power of Germany's war potential and weakening of the German Air Force to the point where it could not hinder the Allied invasion.

On the other hand, if Hitler could successfully employ new weapons before the invasion could be launched, it was possible that 'Overlord', the great cross-Channel operation, could never be executed. The Allied Air Forces, already committed to the greatest task ever given to air power, were therefore called upon to accomplish an additional objective.

Although the British public were informed by the radio and in their newspapers that bombing raids were constantly being carried out all over Europe, they knew nothing of the specific campaign directed against the V-weapon launching sites during the winter and spring of 1943–4. However, Winston Churchill in his typical forthright way gave a clue to what lay ahead, and in particular the threat of a totally new form of warfare, when he addressed Parliament about the state of the war on 22 February 1944. He told MPs and the nation: 'There is no doubt that the Germans are preparing on the French shore new means of attack on this country, either by pilotless aircraft, or possibly rockets, or both, on a considerable scale. We have long been watching this with the utmost vigilance.'

INTRODUCTION

Once again the great statesman had spoken words that were to prove very prophetic. In fact, the opening chapter of 'The Flying Bomb War' was now only a matter of weeks away...

Part I
THE FLYING BOMB

On the night of 12 June 1944, six days after the invasion of France, there appeared over Southern England a new object in the sky. It dashed northward like a flaming meteor over the rich hayfields and ripening cherry orchards of Kent, startled even the war-hardened citizens of that county into leaping out of bed and watching its fiery passage across the midsummer sky, caused a company of staid night-duty policemen at Croydon to stand and cheer like schoolboys under the mistaken impression that a German aircraft was on fire, and finally landed on a bridge in Bethnal Green, London. Next morning the British public knew no more about it than they could read into a dry communiqué recording that a single enemy raider had been shot down over the London area. But in official places, in the War Office, Air Ministry, Home Office, in intelligence rooms of those Commands responsible for the defence of Great Britain, there was full knowledge of what this object was, where it came from and what it could do. There was no illusion about the fact that this, at last, was the Hitler secret weapon, long-trumpeted and long-expected: the pilotless flying bomb, the thing, as a Cockney lady afterwards commented, that 'ain't quite human'. The Wellsian dream of robot flying come true.

H E Bates
Unpublished essay, 1945

The Mystery V-1 of Fareham

Although the British Government maintained a veil of secrecy about its knowledge of the V-1 and V-2 weapons during the spring of 1944, alert newspaper readers were presented with a hint of what lay in store for the nation as early as Friday, 12 May when a number of the daily newspapers carried a short but intriguing report of a very strange aircraft which had crashed in Sweden. The previous day, the *Daily Mail* stated, a 'Nazi mystery plane' had come down in the neutral country and was said to be 'a radio-controlled bomber without a crew and carrying two magnetic mines', though these had luckily not exploded on impact. According to the *Daily Sketch*, the plane was said by eyewitnesses to have been a completely new type, either radio- or rocket-driven, which had suddenly materialised over the country, 'at a great speed with a buzzing sound unlike any usual aircraft drone'. This sound was said to have stopped as the machine fell to earth.

But it was the report in the *Daily Express* which, though the shortest, was actually the most important, for it was the first to use what would soon become a familiar term, 'flying bomb', about this mystery aircraft. Headlined FLYING BOMB FALLS ON SWEDEN, the report, dated Stockholm, Thursday, said: 'A German plane, reported shot down in Sweden, is now rumoured to be a radio-controlled "flying bomb" with which the Germans have been experimenting in the Baltic.' Juxtaposed with this item on the *Express*'s front page was another interesting story, MYSTERY LIGHTS, which reported some equally curious activities in the skies just across the Channel in occupied France. The piece stated: 'Early yesterday and late last night mysterious orange and red lights appeared in the Straits sky which danced about and dived at tangents before falling suddenly.'

Both of these reports hinting at German experiments close at hand at a time when history has subsequently shown that the V-1 was being made operational, take on a special significance when considering the mystery of what a number of people believe to have been the first V-1 to hit England *at least two weeks* prior to the generally accredited opening salvo. It is a mystery story that I have endeavoured to unravel in this first section.

One of the unresolved mysteries of the start of The Flying Bomb War is whether a lone missile was fired from France on 29 May 1944 and exploded just before midnight on the little Hampshire community of Sarisbury Green, close to the town of Fareham, and thereby predated the generally accepted first salvo of flying bombs by over a fortnight. And if it did, *why* the facts were immediately suppressed by the authorities and have remained a secret ever since.

Today there is neither physical evidence in Sarisbury nor official documents in Whitehall to resolve this puzzle, but the rumour persists in local gossip and has at least one outspoken champion who is in no doubt about the evidence he saw with his own eyes.

Although in the spring of 1944 no one in Britain was aware of the fact, it is now clear that Hitler had hoped his Revenge Weapons would have begun their raids against England at some time during the winter, and that 15 February had been specially earmarked for the first mass bombardment of London. But when delays occurred in getting the launching ramps on the Pas de Calais in northern France operational – due in no small measure to the persistent and successful bombing raids of the RAF – this date had to be revised to 20 April. It was a day chosen with particular care by the German High Command and received warmly by the Führer – for it was his birthday!

The Germans also had very good reasons for suspecting at this time that an invasion was being planned against them, and that many of these preparations, such as the assembly of shipping, could not be dispersed but had, in fact, to be concentrated. And this was undoubtedly the reason why numbers of the flying bomb ramps in northern France were pointed not just towards London, but also in the direction of Plymouth, Portsmouth and Southampton.

None of the German military hierarchy were in any doubt that these major ports would be used as invasion bases. And it is not difficult to see that if the harbours had been bombarded by the V-1s in all weathers, night and day, throughout the early months of 1944, they would have created serious obstacles to the invasion plans. As it was, the D-Day landings in Normandy came and went without sight or sound of the dreaded *Vergeltungswaffe* over England.

Or did it? For the evidence from Fareham suggests that one *did* actually reach its target on Whit Monday, 29 May. Whether, though, this flying bomb was a solo launch or had been part of a salvo there is now no way of knowing, but the story of the forerunner of what was to become an aerial armada of death and destruction still makes intriguing reading.

The British Government had, of course, been aware of the threat posed by the V-1 since the previous year and had already issued strict guidelines to the Civil Defence forces about reporting what might at first sight appear to be 'crashed aircraft' which exploded on impact. They wanted no panic among the population if, and when, these secret weapons arrived; but, more importantly, they were anxious that the Germans should have as little idea as possible as to *where* they were landing. The smallest clue would obviously be of paramount importance in establishing the range and distance the flying bombs were achieving.

An extract from a directive issued by the Ministry of Information to British newspaper editors at this time – a copy of which is still on file in the War Museum – provides a fascinating insight into what is a covert act of censorship.

It is particularly important to deny to the enemy any information about the accuracy of his new weapons, and for this reason the normal rule allowing general indications of the location of a raid or incident, i.e. Home Counties, London or London area (including the term 'outskirts' and 'suburbs' of London), S.E., S., S.W., will, so far as raids in Southern England are concerned, be suspended for the time being and only the general term Southern England will be allowed in stories of raids or incidents, including the sounding of an Alert, in any of these areas.

The full directive is, typically, a bit long winded, but the message and its import are clear: one careless word that a flying bomb had fallen within, say, a few miles of two major invasion ports such as Portsmouth and Southampton, could have the most far-reaching effects.

The town of Fareham lies almost equidistant between Portsmouth and Southampton, and it was at nearby Sarisbury Green – the story goes – that the first flying bomb struck two weeks before the widely credited opening shot landed at Gravesend on 13 June.

Today's visitor to the town discovers that the centre is a picturesque collection of Georgian houses clustered around a quiet backwater of the Solent. The area, indeed, mirrors the fact that from the Middle Ages to Victorian times Fareham was a market town and small port which later became a fashionable residence for naval officers. Although there has been much suburban development in the vicinity in recent years, it still offers tourists the unrivalled attraction of

Portsdown Hill which provides one of the finest panoramic views in southern England, for from this point it is possible to see the English Channel, Spithead, much of the Solent and the entire Portsmouth Royal Naval Base.

Sarisbury, a short drive to the west of Fareham, faces the Hamble river, and has been described as an area no longer country but not yet town. A mixture of Victorian cottages and suburban development, its most striking landmark is the church of St Paul, while Sarisbury Green is probably its only focal point.

It was, in fact, beside this green which was once a part of sprawling Titchfield Common and is now ringed with modern houses, that the first V-1 is believed to have fallen. Viewed nowadays as an open space prepared for cricket and frequented by walkers and children playing, there is scant evidence of such an event – but nevertheless the story persists.

The older people who were living here during World War II will tell you that they knew only too well they were uncomfortably close to both Portsmouth and Southampton whenever the German bombers came on raids. And they remember, too, that Southampton, which served as the main port for sending supplies and reinforcements to the Allied Forces in Normandy, not surprisingly became one of the prime targets for the V-1s. On one day alone – I was reminded by a resident as we strolled across the green – Southampton was hit by no less than fifty of the missiles.

But no one had an inkling of this devastation when the bomb which might well have been targeted for either of the two ports went astray and fell on Sarisbury Green on the evening of that early Spring Bank Holiday, Whit Monday.

It had been a really warm day along Southampton Water, folk recall, and if there was a sense of something big in the air, people tried not to raise their hopes too much by saying anything. The invasion of occupied France would come when the generals were good and ready, they told themselves, and grabbed a few hours of relaxation while they waited. Even so, there were those who insisted the big one was now only days away...

The crucial events in the story of the Sarisbury Green flying bomb began as midnight was nearing. The Green itself was deserted, virtually all the houses in total darkness, and the only sign of activity was in a Civil Defence warden's post near the road leading to Park Gate. In the hut, a couple of men on night duty were brewing up for their mid-watch cuppa. Just a few yards away, sombre in the shade of a row of trees, stood a line of tanks waiting to be moved on for embarkation at Southampton.

Suddenly, the stillness was broken by the sound of a strange whining noise in the sky which seemed to be approaching from the direction of the Solent. A few moments later, a small trail of light was visible and what looked like the outline of a small aircraft became distinguishable against the night sky.

Before either of the wardens had time to get their binoculars trained on the intruder, however, an eerie silence fell over the Green. It was followed by a terrific crash and an immediate explosion among the tanks.

Then silence fell once more...a silence that has enveloped the incident and everything that happened at Sarisbury Green from that day to this. What damage was done to the tanks or the surrounding property, whether any civilians were killed or injured by the blast, even if the two wardens survived, has remained a total mystery.

There is, though, one man who is convinced that it *was* a flying bomb that fell that night. His name is Mr B W Rands and he lived in Fareham and was also on duty for the Civil Defence at the very same time. But despite his unshakeable conviction, Mr Rands feels that the secrecy which surrounded the crash on the Green was probably necessary. What he has always wanted is for the record to be put straight. In 1974 he made the following statement which no one either locally or in authority has refuted:

34

'Official records state that the first V-1 to explode on British soil was at Swanscombe near Gravesend on 13 June 1944,' Mr Rands says. 'But I suspect the Official Record is incomplete for an understandable reason. I believe a doodlebug exploded in Hampshire long before 13 June.

'I was on duty in the control room at Fareham on Whit Monday, 1944,' he continues. 'The hour before midnight was still warm after a hot day and there being no "Red" alert we enjoyed the fresh air outside the doorway.

'The sound of a plane with an engine making an unusual noise was heard and then something came into view that appeared to have its tail on fire. Moments after it passed over there was an explosion.

'Wardens' post messages came in of a crashing plane, the crucial one coming from the post at Park Gate, Sarisbury Green, that a plane had crashed on the tanks parked at the roadside and there were casualties. Services were despatched and the incident reported to Regional Headquarters.

'However, almost at once the Military took over and supplanted the Civil Defence. And in the early hours of the next morning Region instructed me to delete from copies of all control-room messages every reference to "plane" and substitute "bomb".

'I argued on the evidence of my own eyes but was told that this was an order from Whitehall and was to be obeyed. Later I was convinced I was right and it dawned on me that the secrecy was to deny the Nazis knowledge as to the range and direction of the doodlebug.'

In hindsight, the account by Mr Rands of the first V-1 over English skies could be said to be as important in its way as Constance Babington Smith's identification of the prototype flying bomb on its ramp at Peenemünde. But the evidence suggests the authorities decided the time was not right for any such news to be made public... especially with D-Day so close. And arguably, of course, they were right.

But this said, the few remaining residents of Sarisbury Green who remember the story of the night the first doodlebug fell on them do believe they deserve at least a mention in the history of the Second World War. Perhaps even a footnote in the story of the evolution of the space rocket...

The Divers are Coming!

There is no argument about the fact that four V-1s reached England in the early hours of Tuesday, 13 June, and thereby heralded the start of the flying bomb war. The first of these pilotless aircraft fell at Swanscombe, near Gravesend at 4.13 a.m.; the second seven minutes later at Cuckfield in Sussex; the third on London itself at 4.25 a.m. near the railway line at Grove Road, Bow; and the final missile half an hour later at Platt, near Sevenoaks, Kent, at 5.06 a.m.

The nation itself had just enjoyed a very pleasant Monday, a day of clear skies and sunshine, savouring news of the Allied Forces' advance in France where, it was said, a coastal strip of 60 miles had been taken and Winston Churchill and General Eisenhower had just visited the Normandy beachhead to see the progress of the invasion for themselves. One newspaper also reported that during the evening a brief rainshower in the Channel had produced a brilliant rainbow over the Straits of Dover and wondered – ironically as events were to turn out in the next few hours – whether this might be a sign of peaceful times ahead!

While work continued as usual in the nation's offices and factories, lovers of horse racing were beginning to pick their favourites for Saturday's Derby, and cricket enthusiasts were following the early season fortunes of Cambridge University playing the Public School Wanderers. In London, the cinemas were drawing good crowds to see David Niven in *The Way Ahead*, Gary Cooper in *For Whom the Bell Tolls* and the continuing success of *Gone With The Wind*. A number of the theatres were likewise doing good business with shows such as Jack Hulbert and Cicely Courtneidge in *Something in the Air* (at the Palace), Naunton Wayne in his second year of *Arsenic and Old Lace* (the Strand), and J B Priestley's new comedy, *How Are They At Home?* (the Apollo).

The Monday evening had also seen the opening at the Lyric of Ronald Miller's highly topical (and in hindsight very aptly titled) play, *Zero Hour* with Hartley Power and Victoria Hopper. But for those who preferred to stay at home, the evening's radio programmes had included a discussion on the latest call for 'Equal Pay for Equal Work' for men and women; a programme of Dinah Shore gramophone records; and half an hour of cheerful tunes by the man whose music somehow epitomised the British spirit during the Second World War, Sandy Macpherson at his organ.

The man who saw the very first of the four 'Divers' to cross the English coast, Arthur Geering, the head of the Royal Observer Corps post at Dymchurch, Kent, had actually been listening to that Sandy Macpherson programme. It was to prove the last undisturbed night he and his wife would enjoy for several months. Arthur later recalled the moment he saw the V-1 in these words: 'It was a week after D-Day when the first of those Divers came over from France. My house faces out across the Romney Marshes to the Kent coast, and it was just after four o'clock on the morning of 13 June when my wife suddenly woke me up. She said she could hear an aircraft outside making an odd noise.

'I got out of bed straightaway and went to the window. I could see this aircraft in the half-light and immediately thought, "Cor – he's got an engine on fire", thinking that what I could see was an ordinary plane. I decided to ring my post, Mike Two, at Dymchurch.

'Another post at Folkestone, D Two, apparently also thought there was a crippled plane coming in, and the ROC Centre at Maidstone asked my post if they could see it. Our two chaps on duty, Archie Wright and Ernie Woodland, had a wonderful pair of American naval binoculars, and as soon as Archie got them trained on the aircraft he immediately put out the code word "Diver"!

'At the Centre, one of the girls said to her Supervisor, Mike Two says they've got a "Diver" and he said, "For Christ's sake push it through, then." She did, but Headquarters didn't believe it to start with. They said that if a flying bomb had been launched from France they would have known about it.

'Well, they soon knew about it a few minutes later when the first one fell near Gravesend! I saw a copy of the report to the Ministry of Home Security which said that it fell on a field growing young greens and lettuces just north of the A2 Rochester-Dartford road. They said it made a crater about twenty feet wide which looked like a saucer, and destroyed all the crops for about eighty yards all around.

'There was also a house nearby which was damaged by the blast, but no one inside was injured. It seemed like a bit of an anticlimax to us after what we had been told to expect, but we didn't know until later that one of those first flying bombs had fallen in London, doing a lot of damage, killing six people and injuring a lot more.

'Of course, we were sworn to secrecy about anything we saw and for a while the radio and papers just talked about enemy raiders being brought down or crashing. By the time they did call them flying bombs they were coming over in droves, all making that terrible noise, and keeping us on the go day and night.'

The British press had also, of course, been sworn to secrecy, and the first report of the V-1 attack to be published in the Tuesday afternoon edition of the London *Evening Standard* made no mention of flying bombs whatsoever:

RAIDER DOWN IN EAST LONDON

A very small force of German aeroplanes spread over East Anglia and south and south-east England during Monday night. People living in London and along the Thames Estuary heard the alert twice in the early hours of the morning. There was a certain amount of gunfire and one raider was brought down in east London. Part of the wreckage fell on the railway line and the L.N.E.R. announce that some passenger services are being diverted until the damage has been repaired. A few bombs which fell in the night caused some damage and a small number of casualties.

In fact, the spot where the first flying bomb to reach London fell was Grove Road in Bow, and it made 200 people homeless as well as causing six deaths and thirty injuries. It also completely blocked a major road and the railway line into Liverpool Street Station. Today the site is marked by a GLC blue plaque which was unveiled in June 1985. At this ceremony, a local man who survived the event, 65-year-old Alfred Mason, recalled how close he came to losing his life when the flying bomb exploded:

'I was in bed and I heard the sirens going in the early hours,' he said. 'But I was one of those cheeky ones and I couldn't be bothered to get out of bed. It was a funny sound and at first I thought it was an airplane. Then it went quiet and the next thing I knew my bedroom walls blew in. I was buried under the rubble for hours before they finally got to me. After that, I never thought it was funny when I heard one of them bloomin' things coming over us!'

Things That Go Whump
in the Night

Among the teeming population of London who watched the arrival of the first flying bombs over the city was the popular novelist, A P Herbert, who was then serving as a Naval Petty Officer and was on board his motor launch, the *Water Gipsy*, in the Thames Estuary, when the first V-1s appeared overhead. That very night, he began to keep a 'Doodlebug Log' about 'the things that go whump in the night', recording his emotions and the reactions of those around him as this wholly new form of death and destruction rained down from the skies.

Although neither A P Herbert – nor anyone else for that matter – knew the actual figures at the time, the Germans followed up their initial four flying bombs with a much more concentrated attack beginning just before midnight on Thursday, 15–16 June. In all, they launched 244 missiles over the Channel, of which 45 crashed soon after launching, several dozen disappeared en route, but 73 got through to the Greater London area providing a night the likes of which the metropolis and its people had never experienced before.

The first night of the doodlebug was the most colourful and crazy scene I remember in the war. A day or two earlier the enemy had sent over a few experimental monsters, one of which fell not far from Gravesend.

This, for good reasons, no doubt, was kept from the people, and even from the commanders of patrol-boats. But one of my former officers, then stationed at Tilbury, gave me a confidential whisper about what we had to expect. Dutiful but wondering, I said no word to my crew.

We were at Tilbury, acting as temporary handmaid to Commander Chapple and his three North Sea trawlers. These were a kind of bomb-and-mine disposal flotilla, ready to fish up anything from anywhere with all the arts of the fishing fleet. He and his three skippers, all from Grimsby, I think, gathered round a little rum, were about the best company in the river. The gallant bomb-fishers were very fond of cockles; we fetched them sackfuls from the Holehaven sands – or wire or warps, whatever they wanted. Now they were after a Mosquito which had plunged with all her bombs into the river below Tilbury. They never found her, but they caught all manner of things. Time and again we watched while the winches rattled and puffed, and the tough trawler heeled over heavily, and some great thing came slowly up to her side. Sometimes it was a vast anchor: twice, as it broke surface, it looked enough like a bomb – a round and shining section of a huge and ancient tree-trunk, as black as coal, and nearly coal itself.

That night, when the sirens sounded, we were anchored below the landing-stage, just above the 'World's End' tavern and Queen Elizabeth's Fort. It was a perfect spot for that obscene spectacle. We could see the little lights appearing, far off, like fireflies, over the Kentish hills: and the unprecedented monsters roared in procession over our heads, for London. Everything in the river (except the *Water Gipsy*) let off everything it had – steamers, mine-sweepers, patrol-boats, all. Sailing bargemen fired their rifles. The river seemed to go mad in the face of this new madness. The Bofors Battery, on the north shore near to us, made a noise like a destroyer in action, and the men were yelling. The red 'tracer' bullets chasing the pale green speeding lights from every part of the wide reach made a fantastic picture. Brock's have never done anything better. As the guns on the south side lowered their trajectory in pursuit of the fleeing targets they seemed to be shooting just over our heads, and I feared for our lives. But nothing of that sort mattered. Tom Cheesman was itching to blaze away with his Hotchkiss like the rest, and could not understand why I restrained him, till I began to disclose my suspicions about the beastly things.[1] Even then, as they roared over, I felt guiltily that I might be betraying a confidence, and, perhaps, ruining the cunning plans of the High Command. One of the things came down in, or near, the Tilbury Docks, and all the sailors cheered like mad. I said, 'I'm afraid that's what they want,' and felt like a killjoy. I wished, indeed, that I had never heard that 'confidential whisper': for everyone else was having fun. It was like a rat hunt. And we were the only dog on the chain.

I wonder how much ammunition was vainly spent that night. And what fools all those eager gunners must have felt next day, when they were told that it was futile and forbidden to fire at the monsters! I assume, respectfully and politely, that the reticent Authorities knew best in this affair; and, one day, I hope to hear what exactly was in their minds.

The next day we were summoned up to London, very sad to leave our trawler friends, and for the following weary weeks we continued to have good views of doodlebugs. All London's citizens think that they saw

---

1 The log reveals our natural bewilderment: '0020 Fifth Mysterious Episode – White light moving target; 0030 something (plane or secret weapon) came over river from S. Great bombardment from all sides. Passed over us, came down N. and exploded. Cheesman thought he saw a parachute. Fred thought it was a Dornier 217. Activity continued all night. Explosions as late as 0745.'

the one which was different from all the others; but that very night I really believe that we met, and avoided, the unique V-1. We went up by night, and about 0200, the flood finished, we tied up to some barge-roads a little upstream from Ford's factory at Dagenham, but on the other side of the river. Before the 'watch below' could turn in, one of the Things came roaring and glowing up from Tilbury towards us, and we all waited on the bridge to see it go over. But, some way short of us, the monster's light went out and the engine stopped. 'Boys!' I remember yelling, 'it's a by-election!' We all scrambled below and lay flat on our stomachs, expecting the worst. Nothing happened: and presently, incredulous, I heard the noise of an engine again. I clambered out on to the bridge, and there, astern of us now, was the Thing in full flight again, light and all, as if it had taken a good look at the *Water Gipsy* and decided to go for bigger game. It roared away and came down about two miles off in the Barking area. I have heard no other tale as tall as this: but I swear that it is true.

Another eyewitness at Tilbury was Keith Scott, then a youngster, who still clearly remembers watching the flying bombs coming over his home at East Tilbury with a mixture of excitement and fear.

'To begin with we thought that the Buzz-Bombs, as we called them, were being aimed at the Tilbury Docks and the oil storage tanks,' he told me. 'So we somehow never thought they might fall on our homes – until they did!

'I remember one night early on when a number of the bombs came over Tilbury. My mother was busy in the kitchen making some jam sandwiches for us to take into the air raid shelter in case we got hungry during the raid. Even when we could actually hear them and my dad was telling her to hurry up she still insisted on finishing the job!

'After the Buzz-Bombs had fallen, my friends and I used to go scrabbling about in the debris looking for bits of them.

Quite a lot of kids collected them and it was always interesting to compare the different parts you found. I suppose going near those ruined buildings was dangerous, but we just thought of it as a bit of a game.

'In fact, the people of Tilbury, like those in London and elsewhere, would just dust themselves down after each V-1 raid and get on with it!'

A Nightmare of
Mortar and Dust

It was not only the centre of London that was hit during the
V-1 onslaught of June 15–16; outlying boroughs such as
Croydon were also struck by a number of flying bombs.
Croydon, in fact, was to find itself a constant target during the
entire period of the raids, earning the unenviable title of 'The
Worst Hit Borough in Greater London'. The reason for this
can now be easily explained: the German launchers in France
consistently underestimated the distance of their main target,
Central London, a fact substantiated by the statistics that the
vast majority of V-1s fell to the south of the Thames in places
such as Camberwell, Woolwich, Wandsworth, Lewisham and
Croydon. It has been estimated that a total of 141 flying bombs
fell on this borough, over 30 more than Lewisham and double
the number which hit such metropolitan centres as
Greenwich and Lambeth. A remarkable account of the first of
the many attacks on Croydon was written by a member of the
Croydon Civil Defence Corps, and this anonymous hand-
written document is still in the possession of the Town
Council. It is a moving report of events that were to be
repeated time and again in the district and describes in the
most personal terms the impact of the V-1 on the lives of
ordinary men and women in wartime England.

The deep-throated roar was heard first. A blinding
flash followed and an explosion that rocked the

warden's post; the projectile had fallen, as was soon discovered, at the junction of Avenue and Warminster Roads. The race to the scene was through a nightmare fog of mortar and dust, the road being carpeted with leaves, glass and rubble. Injured and uninjured were rushing out, dazed and bewildered, in the dim dawn light. The scene itself was desolation; four large houses which were known to be occupied were down and dozens of others were sagging or broken in various ways, and in most of them were people to be helped. A rapid reconnaissance enabled express messages to be sent to the Control for aid. But within a few minutes, there had come soldiers from the searchlight site at South Norwood Club and almost immediately after a party of the Bedfordshires, who were billeted in Auckland Road. They went at once to the work of releasing the trapped; work in which they were joined without delay by a Light Rescue Party which, in good neighbourly fashion, had come over the Penge boundary. There was fortunately no fire to be quenched although the N.F.S. arrived almost at once. There was danger from leaking water in a basement where a casualty was trapped, as so often happened, and the water repair party was summoned. Almost immediately too, came the Housewives Service of the W.V.S. and established their post in a broken garage where with their customary tact and sympathy they did much to help and to comfort anxious enquirers after relatives. Others soon to arrive were the Chief Warden and Bomb Reconnaissance Officer, who, at the seat of the burst, examined the fragments that remained of the new missile in the necessary effort to ascertain its character. Meanwhile, the wardens had worked strenuously to clear the quantities of obstructive broken glass and rubble to enable the ambulances to reach the victims who were being rescued. The latter were speedily recorded and hastened to hospital.

Day was now breaking and, hidden by the low cloud, more flying bombs could be heard hurrying on their errands of destruction, occasionally so near that their engines beat upon the eardrums and this, with the gunfire, produced a confused sense of continuous danger. An elderly lady trapped in an upstairs room was brought out gently and with great difficulty, for the greater part of the big old-fashioned house, including the stairs, had crumbled and she had been found precariously placed on a floor sagging and tied only by one side to the main structure. A crippled and indignant gentleman, marooned in an upstairs room, provided a problem for the Incident Officer as he refused to be removed through the window, even though the stairs were no longer there. People were brought out unhurt from under a Morrison shelter with the house a mound of rubble on top of it.

Seven o'clock came and all the casualties had been cleared but to make sure the whole party, wardens, soldiers and Home Guard, scoured every corner. The residents still in their damaged homes used what resources remained to them to provide welcome tea for the workers.

In retrospect, strange little recollections stand out – the unbelievably dishevelled appearance of a gentleman, smothered from head to foot with soot, plaster, etc. – asleep in an upstairs room; the complete roof had fallen in on him and the whole of the front of the house had fallen out – how he ever managed to find the pair of trousers and shirt in which he appeared, it is doubtful if he will ever know. Cats, not a few but dozens, roaming the ruins of what were once their comfortable homes. The neighbours, who were able to remain, rose to the occasion and set out food and drink for them until such a time as arrangements could be made for their welfare. The elderly lady in night attire, shocked but otherwise unhurt, who lay on a stretcher, cheerful but adamant that she would not be moved to hospital until there should be some news of her husband who had not been under the Morrison with her, but had yet to be recovered from some other part of the ruins of their collapsed home – a happy ending here, he was rescued with only slight injuries. The precise young woman, who troubled to walk from the extreme edge of the damaged area to say to the Incident Officer, 'I have a broken window, have I to report it or something?' and this at the height of the rescue work. And at a later incident, the distinguished gentleman, buried under his house, but dug for and released after more than an hour by toiling rescue workers – who, when carried to his wife and daughter, who had been rescued earlier and in night attire, swathed in eiderdowns and blankets, sat awaiting his release, remarked, 'My dears, I fear we are hardly looking our best.' Trees which a moment before had been in full leaf, the very embodiment of life, now standing bare, twisted and broken, every vestige of green torn from them, their fruit and foliage forming a verdant but bruised carpet, which gave forth a distinctive odour. But above all, the sympathy and help on all sides, our national tendency to insularity knocked out of us with one big sobering bang.

A Croydon builder, John Franklin, whose house was damaged in this attack, was one of the first members of the public to describe a V-1 in flight in an account he gave to a reporter from the *News Chronicle*. Mr Franklin's comments appeared in the issue of Saturday, 17 June beneath what was also the first flying bomb cartoon of the war, 'Planeless Pilots' by Vicky.

'When I first caught sight of the plane it appeared to be flying at about 300–400 miles per hour and at a height of 2,000 feet,' he said. 'In size it was rather less than half that of a Spitfire, but it had no propeller or tailplane.

'It was losing height gradually. Flashes about half the length of the fuselage were coming out behind it; they were reddish-yellow in colour and spat backwards at intervals of about five seconds.

'Soon after the plane passed over my head its engine cut out and the flashes stopped at the same time. It did a half-turn, then went into a steep dive.

'It crashed through the top of a roof opposite my own house and then a few seconds later blew up in the road. It seemed to be all surface blast,' Mr Franklin added.

Pilotless Warplanes
Raided Britain

This was the newspaper headline in inch-high letters – repeated in the strident cries of sellers – which started a rush for copies of the *Evening News* when its first editions appeared on the streets of London and the south east on Friday, 16 June carrying the report hereunder. Already, of course, there were many people in the city and scattered about the southern counties who had felt the impact of the terrible new German weapon, but this was the first time the facts had been confirmed in print – and on no less authority than that of Herbert Morrison, the widely respected Home Secretary and Minister of Home Security.

Morrison, the son of a Lambeth policeman, who had risen to the top in politics because of his no-nonsense approach and close affinity with the people, had never doubted the frightening potential of the Nazi V-weapons. In the preceding year he had fought to maintain the number of Civil Defence workers in the likelihood of a new German attack on the country and was pleased at the success of the indoor anti-bomb shelter which bore his name and looked to all intents and purposes like a fortified kitchen table! Even with D-Day having triumphantly come and gone, the Home Secretary's conviction that the flying bombs would still be launched was totally vindicated – but he took no pleasure in rising before the House of Commons on the morning of 16 June to reveal to the nation the danger it was facing.

Last night's raid on Southern England was made by pilotless German aircraft and more raids are expected, announced Mr Morrison in the House of Commons today. While awaiting full reports of their effect, he warned the public not to stay in the streets out of curiosity if our AA guns open up in daylight.

On the other hand these new nuisance attacks need not be exaggerated. Countermeasures are being applied with full vigour and meanwhile the usual siren warning will continue.

Mr Morrison's statement began: 'It has been known for some time that the enemy was making preparations for the use of pilotless aircraft against this country and he has now started to use this much-vaunted new weapon. A small number of these weapons were used in raids on Tuesday morning and their fall was scattered over a wide area. A larger number was used last night and this morning.

'On the first occasion the attack was slight and caused a few casualties and the damage was on the whole inconsiderable. But last night's attack was more serious and I have not yet full particulars of casualties and damage or the number of pilotless aircraft destroyed before any could explode.

'The enemy's preparations have not, of course, passed unnoticed and countermeasures have been and will be applied with full vigour. It is probable, however, such attacks will continue and subject to experience, the usual siren warning will be given.'

Mr Morrison added that it was important not to give the enemy any information in directing his shooting by telling him where his missiles had landed.

'It may be difficult', he said, 'to distinguish these from ordinary air raids. Therefore it has been decided that information published about the air raids in southern England south of the line from the Wash to the Bristol Channel will not give any indication where the raid has taken place beyond saying that it occurred in southern England.

'While I have thought it right to inform the House at the first opportunity about the new weapon used by the enemy, the available information does not suggest that exaggerated importance need be attached to this new development. All possible steps are being taken to frustrate the enemy's attempts to supplement nuisance raids by means which do not imperil the lives of his pilots.

'Meanwhile the nation should carry on its normal business, but as, however, the raids by pilotless planes may occur also in daylight when the streets are full of people and the AA guns may be shooting, I must impress upon the public the importance of not exposing themselves to danger in the streets out of curiosity.

'Perhaps I might add that for the time being at any rate the guns will shoot. But that is liable to review as we go along in the light of experience and what is expedient.'

Mr Morrison said members would notice the arrangements made with the Press to avoid the enemy learning where his pilotless aircraft are falling. He was sure that if members had any questions they put down, and particularly in oral supplementaries and observations, they would themselves act up to the practices which we have asked the Press to observe.

Mr Stokes (Lab., Ipswich) asked if it was the intention to continue warnings at the present, irrespective of whether they were piloted or pilotless planes. If that was done, he said, it might mean that large numbers of people would stay in their houses unnecessarily.

Mr Morrison: 'It is my intention to treat both in the same way at the present, but there is a point in what you say. In all these matters we have to learn as we go along, and I shall not hesitate to modify the system if, in the public interest, it becomes expedient to do so.'

Mr Anthony Eden (Leader of the House): 'It will be the desire of the House that we should continue business each day without interruption. In order to enable us to do so – should there be a warning – it is necessary formally to move the suspension of one of our Orders which would bring business to an end if there were a warning. I move therefore that the order of the House dated 24 November 1943 relative to its sittings be suspended during the day's sittings.' The motion was agreed to.

An *Evening News* reporter writes: It should not be long before our war scientists and the RAF take the full measure of the German pilotless bomber. We have known for a long time that the enemy had this type of plane up his sleeve. That was one of the reasons why the RAF have ruthlessly bombed the Pas de Calais area of the French coast with hundreds of planes for the last six months – for, besides rocket-gun emplacements, radio control bases for such a plane have been the other menace.

We knew that the German threat to hit us with bombers without crews was not an idle threat; that even jet-propulsion might be used; that experiments were conducted only last month in Northern Germany with a machine six to eight yards long, shaped like a bomb, with aileron stabilisers.

Full-sized radio-controlled planes were also tested out by the Germans in April on the Danish island of Bornholm and beam methods of control have also been reported.

One possibility has been that several of these winged bombers, each equipped with a radio set, might be controlled by a 'mother' plane with a human crew.

Germany has been making experiments for years, but so has the RAF with the 'Queen Bee' and other types. They have already used a 'glider bomb' fitted with wings and controlled by their planes against our ships in the Mediterranean.

Alongside this story on the front page, the *Evening News* also printed a guide for its readers to the new German secret weapon which it headlined:

HOW TO SPOT THE GHOST PLANES

Descriptions of the German pilotless planes vary slightly in detail. But they agree on these points – terrific speed, bright lights, flames from exhaust and a very straight course. Our correspondent telephoned this picture of them today:

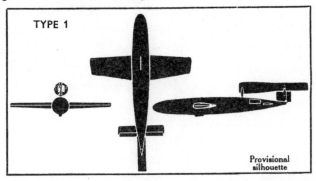

TYPE 1

Provisional silhouette

The planes have a distinctive, rhythmic note, giving the effect of a pulsating low throb. They are much smaller than a Spitfire, but have an appearance much the same.

They are really midget planes. At night they show a distinct yellow glow at the rear, and in the light of searchlights streams of thick smoke can be seen being ejected from them.

Many of them have been observed in daylight and on several occasions RAF fighters, with total disregard of the danger, have dived into the AA fire around them in attempts to make a kill.

They appear to be painted a dark brown or black, the smoke issues from them in small thick puffs, attuned to the throb which can be heard.

They streak across the sky at a very great speed. They appeared to come across the Channel, and it is believed that at times two or three were sent over together.

The Home Security Ministry issued this advice today: 'When the engine of the pilotless aircraft stops and the light at the end of the machine is seen to go out, it may mean that the explosion will soon follow – perhaps in five to fifteen seconds.

'So take refuge from the blast. Even those indoors should keep out of the way of the blast and use the most solid protection immediately available.'

The Propaganda War

The first weekend of the flying bomb attacks saw British and German sources making widely differing claims about their impact on England. For example, *The Times* newspaper, that pillar of the Establishment and paper of record, devoted its main leader on Saturday, 17 June to playing down the impact of the V-1 and urging the nation to be resilient to its threat. But despite the optimistic tone of this column, headlined with characteristic understatement, 'Night Raiding', the paper was mistaken in believing the new weapons to be 'wireless controlled' and to be having no more than a 'nuisance' effect. Nazi propaganda, on the other hand, believed no claim too outrageous to make, stating that their 'Dynamite Meteors', as the V-1 was being described in Germany – had 'set London ablaze'! Although the British Government had ordered its press to keep secret the targets and casualties of the flying bomb, they could hardly have failed to be pleased at the scorn which was poured on the fanciful claims by the German media in syndicated reports such as that from the British United Press agency in neutral Stockholm which appeared in several British papers.

NIGHT RAIDING

The government have wisely taken the nation into their confidence without delay on the subject of the attacks by the so-called new weapons which the Germans launched on Tuesday night and repeated in greater strength on Thursday night and yesterday. The Home Secretary's statement was cool and balanced, and his advice to the public, supplemented by his further announcement last night, should be followed in the spirit as in the letter. The reasons for which all information as to the incidents and effect of the enemy's attack must be withheld are clear and cogent. The new weapon is simply a development of a well-known invention. Pilotless aircraft carrying incendiaries or high explosives are set going from across the Channel. They are directed by wireless control, and eventually the aeroplane falls and explodes. It is obvious that there can be no precision whatever in this form of bombing, and its direction is subject to a very wide margin of errors. Failing the close and frequent observation of the fall of these contrivances – a difficult, hazardous and costly task for the depleted and hard-pressed Luftwaffe of today – it is clearly that of pure chance if the enemy inflicts any military damage whatever by this form of attack. Since he will naturally endeavour to obtain all possible information of its results in order to improve his technique and impart some precision to these missiles, it is essential that he should learn nothing.

Militarily, therefore, the new weapon cannot have the slightest effect on the course of the war. It may inflict a certain degree of loss and injury on the civilian population, but that, so far as can be foreseen, is likely to be limited in its effectiveness, and the damage so far caused is officially described as 'relatively small'. The aim of these nuisance raids is no doubt to shake the morale of the British public, which has never been stronger than today, and to comfort the German people who, with their great industries devastated and with defeat steadily overtaking them on every front, are urged to cling to the hope that some new weapon may save them from the overthrow which they are at last beginning to foresee.

Mr Morrison assured Parliament yesterday that all possible steps are being taken to frustrate the enemy's attempt to execute these raids 'by means which do not imperil the lives of his pilots'; and there is no reason to suppose that the Air Ministry, which has known for some time of the German intention, will fail to devise means to deal with this form of attack. In any case, its continuation must depend on the enemy's ability to maintain his hold on those regions of France which are nearest to this country, a hold which is already threatened and may soon relax as the Allied armies press in from three sides on the encircled Reich.

The Times

LONDON ABLAZE!

The news of Hitler's new secret weapon has crowded the Battle of Normandy off the front pages of the German Press and out of the radio station bulletins this weekend. Fantastic possibilities are foreseen for this pilotless plane. Military commentators are predicting that it will neutralise the allied invasion and could in time drive it back.

The German propaganda machine is squeezing every ounce of value out of the new weapon and is trying to convince the nation's people that with it they can snatch victory from the jaws of defeat. 'Dynamite Meteors' is the term which has been coined for the planes.

The German newspapers announced the first appearance of these pilotless planes with the boldest red headlines. In the case of the *Deutsche Allgemeine Zeitung* these covered a large portion of the front page above a message which stated, 'The Führer had said often and plainly enough that retaliation would come for crimes committed against German civilians. First reports from Britain indicate terrified surprise at the coming of the punishment.'

Another paper, the *Nachtausgabe*, in similar large print declared, 'We give in, in this hour, to feelings of hatred and retaliation against the enemy who wanted to destroy the Germans by terror and unscrupulous barbarity.'

According to these papers, explosions from London were clearly heard on the French coast, while the ruddy skies indicated fires over the whole of the south of England which had been shaken as if hit by an earthquake. The reports claimed that London and the South Coast were now shrouded in a pall of dense smoke that was preventing exact observation by German reconnaissance aircraft.

However, a description of sorts was offered by a Lieutenant Fritz Worschek who said he had flown over London during the night and seen the city ablaze – incomparably worse than Berlin ever was. Indeed, Berlin's worst fires – which Worschek had himself seen – seemed insignificant in comparison to what he had just witnessed over London, he said.

German radio stations have also been pouring out a vast spate of propaganda about the new weapon. It was to be expected that Goebbels would dress it up in the most fantastic way. Reports have been issued by the score that the pilotless planes have caused the war to 'enter a new phase', that they have caused 'unique destruction', 'enormous conflagration', 'incessant explosions', stoppage of work in factory and office, disruptions of communications, closing of shops, panic, etc., etc.

A typical broadcast from a Berlin radio station told listeners, 'The thick oily clouds of black smoke that have been hanging over London during the past few days are proof of the effectiveness of the new German weapon. There are fires everywhere between Kingston and Bromley and smoke miles high over Southampton and Portsmouth.

'The British government has given orders for the immediate evacuation of the population, and many trains with thousands of refugees are leaving for the north. The roads leading from London to the country are also choked with panic-stricken refugees. Seven million Londoners are today forced to resort to camping. Only a few have motors. Most take their pots and pans with them on hand-drawn carts and other improvised vehicles.'

Another German station broadcasting in English to countries outside Europe echoed this unbelievable theme. 'In London life has practically come to a standstill as the rain of secret weapons is continuing almost without interruption. Buckingham Palace has been badly damaged in these raids, but the Royal Family suffered no injury because they had been evacuated to the safety of a secluded castle in Scotland.'

German radio has also been going to great lengths to make clear the impact of these weapons upon their own people. 'Immediately after the announcement that it was in use,' reported one commentator, 'the offices of Berlin newspapers were flooded by telephone calls. In trams, tubes and trains people who did not know one another were all talking about the pilotless planes.'

The daily war report of another station added, 'The news spread like lightning through the positions of our soldiers in Normandy. Every soldier on this front has been perfectly aware that the war had entered a decisive stage. The news caused a tremendous outburst of joy among the soldiers, who have been having a very hard time in standing firm against the hail of enemy fire.'

In response to British press claims on Friday that the RAF had known about the pilotless planes for some time and had diverted fighters to watch for them during the invasion of France, the German press has countered that Berlin allowed the invasion to take place in order to use the bomb.

'The British invading forces,' a statement said, 'were deliberately allowed to land in France in order to enable the robot rockets to be introduced on 15 June so as to cut off Allied communications and supplies and facilitate the destruction of the whole invading Army.'

Politically, it is claimed, the robot has achieved at least one thing and that is to restore confidence in Hitler's leadership and his promise of secret weapons which sane Germans lately doubted.

Yesterday the German press warned its readers against expecting the 'Dynamite Meteors' to decide the war as they cannot be used in Normandy because the effects of their explosions are so great that they could not avoid harming the German defenders in such a confined space.

The weapon is stated, however, to be already seriously influencing the invasion front, against which there is no better target at present than its base, London and the south of England, particularly if London is the focus point for all invasions and the seat of the military invasion staff.

The effect of the explosion of one of these 'Meteors' is claimed to be greater than that caused by a thousand aeroplane attacks. As an illustration of how they are already affecting the front, one Berlin report says that the rations for the troops in Normandy have been reduced by one third since the reprisal campaign against England began and the delivery of munitions has also slackened to an unspecified extent.

Lord Haw-Haw also broadcast about this 'German triumph' on Saturday night (17 June) attempting yet again to convince British listeners of the futility of opposing Hitler.

'There is a general and very natural feeling among the people that the British government has failed seriously in an emergency which ought to have been foreseen. At least Mr Morrison should have been able to state a clear policy in the matter of sirens, although it seems to be a characteristic of this government that it can't state a clear policy on any subject. Mr Churchill ought not only to have foreseen that the Germans would make use of some such weapons, but should also have made sure of adequate countermeasures.'

American listeners were also the target of another of Goebbels' streams of fantasy in a broadcast on Saturday night.

'The night before last,' it stated, 'the US Army suffered the heaviest casualties so far. One of the robot machines crashed into the railroad station in London and exploded just when the station was crowded with US soldiers. It is estimated that between 3,000 and 4,000 US soldiers were killed.

'American Red Cross nurses have stated that some of the US soldiers were torn to pieces so badly that they could not be identified. Soldiers in the US army station in London have also complained bitterly that they are ordered to go out and rescue English civilians while German pilotless aircraft are exploding overhead.'

But even this fantasy was surpassed by another German commentator who suggested that the new weapon, which at present has a range of approximately 150 miles, would eventually be used against New York. He predicted the eventual destruction of all the cities on the Atlantic seaboard of America.

One broadcaster summed up the secret weapon: 'To bomb without motor and without wireless control has many advantages and it is likely that we shall hear much more of these rocket planes.'

The New
Battle of Britain

Despite the claims and counter-claims of the first weekend of the flying bomb attacks, it was, in hindsight, one of the worst in terms of deaths and the destruction of property. By Monday morning, 19 June, it had been estimated that a total of over 500 bombs had been launched at London and the south east, more than 450 people had been killed and over 2,000 injured, while as many as 130,000 houses and buildings had been damaged by the explosions. Without doubt, the worst single incident had been the bomb which scored a direct hit on the Royal Military Chapel at the Wellington Barracks in London while the Sunday morning service was in progress, killing 119 and seriously injuring 102 servicemen and civilians. It was to be three weeks before the Government allowed details of this terrible tragedy to be made public.

If there was any good news that weekend, however, it was the fact that the fighter pilots were beginning to come to grips with the intruders in the air. Ever since the triumph of the Battle of Britain, the RAF had been in control of the skies over Britain – but this new jet-propelled missile provided a serious threat to their authority due to its speed and the danger of explosion when attacked. Because the V-1 was capable of flying in excess of 350 m.p.h. as it neared its target, only the British Spitfires and Tempests and the American Mustangs and Thunderbolts, now based in the country, had sufficient power to catch it and try to knock it out of the sky. The very speed of this new form of aerial warfare also meant that it was difficult for the people of southern England to see what was going on, and there was naturally considerable interest when an RAF spokesman, Squadron Leader John Strachey, gave the following revealing – and reassuring – talk on the BBC's Home Service on 26 June.

The question of the flying bomb is a matter of concern to those of us who live in southern England. They are beastly, vicious things. But don't let us forget what a small part the flying bombs are playing in the whole enormous pattern of events.

In fact, it is not too much to say that from a military point of view the flying bomb is quite negligible. It is militarily negligible, that is to say, at the level of intensity at which the Germans have been able to launch it. I am not saying that *if* the Germans had been able to carry out their original plans, at the time when they had meant to carry them out, they might not have obtained an indirect military effect.

But we had known for a long time about the Germans' plans to make this attack on us. They originally meant to launch the bomb in the spring of 1943, and to launch it from more than a hundred points on the French coast. Their preparations did not go undisturbed.

First attacks were made on the experimental factories at Peenemünde and elsewhere where the flying bomb was being manufactured. Then, beginning last November, tens of thousands of tons of bombs were dropped on the launching points, while they were being built. Every bomb which could be spared from the job of preparing the way for the second front was thrown on to the launching sites. The result was that the attack was delayed for over a year; and now that it has come it is on much less than half the scale on which the Germans originally planned it.

As anyone in southern England can see for themselves, it has proved unable to affect our own land, sea and air attack upon Germany in the least degree. The Germans' propaganda about the bomb has become comic. Did you see, for example, that Goebbels was saying that the first refugees from England had already arrived in France, or better still, that the flying bombs had destroyed 'the great port' of Maidstone?

Though the flying bomb has turned out to be militarily negligible that does not mean that its effect may not often be personally tragic. It is almost unbearably sad, at this late stage of the war, to see again the effect of high explosives on an ordinary street of little houses. Apart from the tragedy of those individuals who are killed or badly hurt, there is all the suffering and pain of smashed homes, lost personal possessions, families broken up – and it is being done by the enemy without any real military purpose at all.

As usual there is not the slightest need for anyone to tell the people of southern England to keep steady. They are steadiness itself. In fact, the main thing that needs saying is once again to urge them to take reasonable and sensible precautions. These, remember, are essentially blast bombs.

We have found that all our standard types of shelters – the Andersons, the Morrisons and the surface shelters – offer good protection against the blast. So get into some kind of shelter if you can when you hear them close by, or at least take the elementary precaution of getting away from the windows: it is flying glass that is one of the main dangers.

There is no need to describe what the flying bomb looks like and sounds like to listeners who live within range. But you in the rest of the country may not realise just what it is like when these things come over.

First you hear a faint humming in the distance, more

or less like an ordinary aircraft. Gradually it grows louder, and the note changes till it sounds more like a motor-bike with a two-stroke engine being driven through the sky. Soon, if it is a clear day, you see the little aircraft, with the hump on its back, flying along a few thousand feet up. If it is at night you see a light, which is the exhaust flame, coming out of the back. The noise grows and grows and if the flying bomb goes right over your head it sounds like an express train dashing through the sky. If the noise stops it means that it will drop and explode in anything from five to fifteen seconds or so. That is the time to get away from the windows and take any other reasonable precautions.

Obviously I cannot describe to you in any detail the countermeasures which we are taking against the flying bombs. The enemy would give a great deal to know about them. They are extensive. We are bombing the launching points: the number which we hit and are put out of action will depend very largely on the weather. Given a few clear days and nights we may be able to do a good deal in that way.

Then again our fighters are shooting them down. Our Spitfires and the American Mustangs and Thunderbolts are getting an increasing bag. Our newest fighter, the Tempest, has proved particularly good at this job. And our gunners are also attacking them.

We must not expect, I think, that these countermeasures will stop the flying bomb altogether in the immediate future. It always takes a little time completely to overcome a new form of attack. But already we have done a good deal to limit the scale of the thing. A lot more is being done.

No doubt the best way to ensure that no more flying bombs ever come over is to capture the places from which they are being fired. After all, we have done that already in the case of the Cherbourg launching points. There were quite a number of launching points at the end of the Cherbourg peninsula, intended, I think, to fire on our West Country towns. They never got a chance to fire at all before the Americans took the peninsula.

What I am getting at is that by preventing the flying bombs from coming over for a year – actually until after our armies had got back into France – the Allied Air Force set a comparatively short limit to the period during which this attack could be made on us. And do not forget that the bombing of Germany is going on all the time.

Neither the attention which we have paid to the launching points of the flying bomb, nor the far, far greater weight of bombs which we have dropped in direct support of the armies, has prevented either the RAF or the American Eighth Bomber Command from continuing the attack on Germany itself: that gives you a sense of the size of the combined air resources which Britain and America command today.

It is interesting to compare the weight of attack which Germany is getting with what we are getting here. In the past twelve days and nights a few hundred flying bombs have been scattered all over southern England. But on Wednesday last the Forts and Liberators put down 1,300 tons of bombs on the railway system in the centre of Berlin in a few minutes, in broad daylight; and that was not their only operation that day. And the day before they had attacked twelve synthetic oil plants and refineries all over central and northern Germany.

The result of these attacks on Germany's oil supply is to deny the once-dreaded Luftwaffe its fuel and make its aircraft as impotent as the flying bombs will soon be!

Irene Cowan of Rochford in Essex was not far from Broadcasting House when she saw her first flying bomb roar overhead. She was seventeen years old and living in

London at the time, and was walking along Regent Street looking in the shop windows when the sound of a V-1 made her look up.

'Everyone stopped when the doodlebug came over,' she told me. 'I could see it quite clearly against the morning sky. It was shaped like a torpedo and there was this flame coming out of the back. The noise it made was dreadful!

'Strangely, I wasn't frightened and I remember marvelling to myself that there was no man inside flying the machine. But when the people around me began running for cover I realised it was dangerous and walked into the nearest shop, which happened to be Dickens and Jones.

'I carried on looking at the goods on the counters and then found something I thought I would buy. I held it out to the assistant behind the counter.

'"I'm sorry, Madam," the man said to me in a very courteous voice as I was digging into my handbag for some money, "but we don't serve anyone when there is an air raid on"!'

The Doodlebug Killer

The arrival of the V-1 over the skies of England presented a totally new challenge to the fighter pilots of the RAF – one which, as has been indicated, they rose to immediately. The pilots did not take long to adopt the nickname 'Doodlebug' for the robot planes in preference to 'Buzz Bomb' which enjoyed a public vogue for a while. This, however, was only when talking about the bombs in public: in the intimacy of the mess they much preferred the more ribald 'Farting Fannies' or 'Hitler's Virgins' – because 'they've never had a man inside them!' to quote one pilot. A certain squadron leader apparently delighted in telling new recruits to his flight that the bombs ran on a completely new type of fuel: Arse-alight!

Competition to shoot down the flying bombs very quickly became as intense as it had been to knock German aircraft out of the skies during the Battle of Britain. The man credited with shooting down the first doodlebug was Flight Sergeant Maurice Rose, a Scotsman from Glasgow, who was a member of 150 Wing in No. 3 Squadron, Fighter Command, led by the legendary Wing Commander Roland Beaumont. The squadron was very much in the front line of the battle against the V-1s, being based at Newchurch near Dungeness, Kent, and in the following account published in the *Empire News* of 20 July 1944, Maurice Rose describes what it was like to confront a robot enemy and the chance that enabled him to score the first victory against one.

The Doodlebug was coming straight out of the sun at my aircraft. Even in the glare I could still see the flame from its motor and the noise of the engine sounded like a motorcycle on the blink.

I am used to facing Hun fighter pilots who always try to come out of the sun at you – but they twist and turn to make it difficult for you to get a clean shot. But this new Nazi terror weapon didn't deviate an inch as it came straight on towards me.

The whole situation seemed crazy, almost unreal. But there was no time to think. I had to set my sights and go into action. I was about to do something no fighter pilot had ever done before. Go into battle against a robot enemy...

Today I can tell you that it was my good fortune to be the first pilot to shoot down a Doodlebug in daylight. And since that morning I have seen quite a lot more of these flying bombs destroyed – although others have unhappily, of course, been able to escape our defences and drop on innocent citizens.

I am sure that most people know that the Doodlebugs do not have a pilot and carry a large amount of explosive which detonates on impact with the target. That unearthly sound which you hear is the jet engine thrusting it forward: when it cuts out the flying bomb plummets down.

It's our job in the RAF to bring down these latest examples of Hitler's callous disregard for the lives of civilian men, women and little children. We have to blow them up before they can do any harm. It is a job that I and all the fighter pilots assigned to the task tackle with a real relish.

I have heard it said that a New Zealand pilot was responsible for giving these weapons the nickname 'Doodlebugs' but someone else told me that in America they have an annoying little insect that flies all over the place bothering people and making a whining noise which is also called a 'doodlebug' – so take your choice!

I also read recently that tackling the flying bombs is said to be rather like 'joining in a very fast game of rugger on a very small ground' and I can certainly vouch for that. For there is not a lot of space for manoeuvring when you are chasing a Doodlebug and trying to keep clear of the barrage balloons and all the ack-ack fire being put up by the anti-aircraft guns below!

As a matter of fact, I was very lucky to get into the battle of the Doodlebugs at all. Three days before I shot that first one down, I was on an offensive patrol in France behind the Allied lines in Normandy when I was hit by a German fighter and had to bail out.

Luckily I landed safely, but now I had no plane to fly. So I was sent back across the Channel in a supply vessel and returned to my base. Soon afterwards, though, I was given my new aircraft, the very latest British fighter, the Hawker Tempest. These are tremendously fast planes and terrific to fly.

It was while I was on my very first flight in the plane, as I was going over the Channel, that I suddenly saw a flying bomb come buzzing towards me. Of course, I had heard about them at briefings but no one had actually seen one in flight before!

But there was no time for getting a close look at this one. I just fixed it in my sights and gave it a full burst with my guns. Fortunately, the thing blew up in mid-air. The whole incident was all over as quickly as that.

Since that first encounter, my squadron has been responsible for bringing down a lot more Doodlebugs, and all the time we have been getting better at the job. The fact that the Tempest is so fast and its guns are so accurate has been a great help to us on our missions.

Let me tell you what it is like to attack a Doodlebug when you have been 'scrambled' from base or if you should suddenly see one while on patrol.

The first thing you hear is the sound like an angry bee and then a tiny speck of light appears over the horizon growing bigger every second. The buzz and the light soon become synchronised into what appears to be a meteor with a flaming orange-red tail.

Sometimes near the coast, ack-ack guns will open up below you and you can see red and white tracer shots streaming up towards the robot. If they hit the intruder all well and good, but if they don't then it becomes your turn to go in. Of course, it has become part of our tactics to attack the robots before they reach the coast so we don't run the risk of being hit by the ack-ack fire ourselves!

As you close up on the robot, it looks rather like a large flame with wings sticking out on either side. Because it is so small, the flying bomb is not easy to hit, but it is still vulnerable. If your bullets strike home on the jet unit, the whole thing catches fire and it goes down with a crash. If you hit the explosives it is carrying, the robot blows up.

When we started attacking these machines we trod warily, shooting from long range, but as we have got experienced at this new form of attack, we have found we can close in, sometimes to 100 yards.

If you are close when the bomb goes up you sometimes fly through the debris, and some of our Tempests have come back with their paint scorched. Some have even been turned on their backs by the force of the explosion, but the pilot feels no effect except an upward jolt.

Often it is not necessary to hit your target cleanly. A few bullets sometimes upset the gyro (automatic pilot) and the robot crashes straight down into the sea. One of our chaps has also discovered that by using his slip-stream it is possible to force the Doodlebugs into a spin.

We are now getting expert at intercepting an increasing number of Doodlebugs, and all this practice is helping to make our shooting very accurate. We are confident in the future of stopping a high proportion of those sent over from the German positions in France. In fact, during one patrol I was in a few days ago we saw seven and bagged the whole lot!

I am certain we shall have a lot more success against these raiders and prove that all Goebbels' claims for them are just so much hot air.

Hunting the Flying
Bombs by Night

The V-1s were not, of course, restricted by the elements like
other aircraft: in fine weather or bad, and by day or night,
they could be launched across the Channel at England.
Attacking them at night was an especially hazardous task
for the RAF pilots and required special training. The man
credited with shooting down the first flying bomb at night
was Flight Lieutenant John Musgrave from Lincolnshire, a
Mosquito pilot of the County of Warwick Squadron.

The pilot who became most famous for his exploits against
the flying bombs at night, however, was Squadron Leader
Joseph Berry, also a member of No. 3 Squadron, who during a
remarkable period to the end of August 1944 shot down sixty
V-1s, all but three at night. Berry, an income tax collector in
Nottingham prior to joining the RAF, won a DFC and Bar in
action over Italy before playing an inspirational role in the
battle against the flying bombs. Piloting a Tempest, his best
'bag' was seven V-1s in a single night. Tragically, in September
1944 with the campaign effectively won and having been
named as the pilot who had destroyed most flying bombs,
Berry was shot down by AA fire while on patrol over the Dutch
coast. As his plane plunged towards the sea, the Squadron
Leader was heard to tell the other members of his flight over
the radio, 'Carry on chaps, I've had it.' He was just twenty-
four. A recording of Berry's voice still exists, however, for a few
weeks before his untimely death he gave a broadcast on the

BBC Home Service about his role in the war against the flying
bombs, part of which is reprinted hereunder.

There are probably those of you among my listeners
tonight who imagine that tackling a robot which cannot
shoot back or take evasive action is, to use a popular
service term, a 'piece of cake'. Nothing could be further
from the truth, I assure you!

As many of you will probably know, the first of these
flying bombs, or 'doodlebugs' as they are popularly
called, were fired at us by the Germans during the
daytime. Our fighter pilots could see them coming and
were able to pick a lot of them off in the air.

Soon the Germans started to send them over at night
when the only thing that was visible were the flames
coming from their jet engines. To start with, some of our
day-fighter pilots were sent to try to intercept the robots.
Normally these pilots in their Tempests and Spitfires are
crack shots, but it soon became apparent that they were
not sufficiently at home in the dark clouds of night.

Because of the urgency of the situation, it was
decided by the RAF top brass to see if some of the night-
fighter pilots could convert to flying the Tempest more
easily than the day-fighter pilots could convert to all-
weather night flying.

There were those who were sceptical about this plan,
I know, because I was one of the night-fighter pilots
involved right from the very start. And because I already
had some experience of attacking the doodlebugs in
daylight, I can tell you that flying against them by night
proved even more dangerous. Fortunately, we became
very successful and are now in a position to tackle the
robots at whatever time they appear in our skies.

Of course, when the first flying bombs came over the
Channel from France in the middle of June, very little
was known about their habits and construction, and all
fighter pilots had to experiment and swop experiences

to work out the best method of destroying them or shooting them down. We had to find out how near we could get to the flying bomb and shoot without the risk of being blown up by it, and I have to tell you that some brave men died before the answer was obtained.

It was on the lawn of a cottage in Southern England close to an airfield that, every evening, one of the most important little councils of war took place during the first stages of the battle with the flying bombs. The cottage was a wing intelligence office, and on its lawn the pilots of a Tempest squadron, led by Wing Commander Roland Beaumont, gathered to compare notes and discuss their experiences. Methods of approaching and attacking the robots would be discussed one evening, tried out the next day during ops, and then reported on that evening.

During this experimental period nobody worked harder than the 'Wing Co' who flew day after day from first light till dusk, and finally the perfect method of attack was evolved – the approach from astern at an acute angle. Results were immediate; the 'bag' went up hand over fist and casualties dropped equally sharply.

They were long summer days for the pilots, some of them frequently spending twenty of the twenty-four hours within sight of their machines. They had to grab some shut-eye whenever they could. But they soon had the satisfaction of using only 150 rounds for each 'doodle' destroyed compared with more than 500 at first.

It was in July that I was posted as a Squadron Leader to organise night-flying against the doodlebugs. Although my squadron had to put up with a lot of leg-pulling in the officers' mess whenever low clouds or rain prevented us from flying, once we were airborne there were usually rich pickings to be had. On 23 July I had the chance to demonstrate how good our technique had become when I shot down seven of these robots in one night!

But don't get the idea that the doodlebug goes down easily. It will take a lot of punishment and the pilot has to aim at the propulsion unit – that's the long stove-pipe, as we call it, on the tail.

If your range and aim are dead on, you can see pieces flying off the stove-pipe. The big white flame at the end then goes out, and down goes the bomb. Sometimes it dives straight to earth, but at other times it goes crazy and gives a wizard display of acrobatics before finally crashing.

Sometimes the bomb explodes in mid-air, and the flash is so blinding that you cannot see a thing for about ten seconds. You hope to be the right way up when you are able to see again, because the explosion often throws the fighter about and sometimes even turns it upside down.

There are a great many things I could tell you that we have learned about fighting the doodlebugs, but there is one more interesting sidelight I should like to add. This is the story of how we have found a way of destroying the flying bombs without even firing a shot.

In a busy sortie, a pilot can quite easily run out of ammunition. One day, a pilot from one of the Polish Squadrons [316 City of Warsaw Squadron – Editor] found he had used up all his ammunition on a group of doodlebugs, but was still on the track of a lone raider. He had a sudden flash of inspiration and flew in alongside the doodlebug. Then by getting his wing tip under that of the robot and giving it an upward flick, he found he could turn it on its back and send it crashing down into the empty countryside below.

This delicate manoeuvre has since been tried out successfully by other fighter pilots, and we have learned that it is even possible to turn the bomb right around and head it back towards its base on the Pas de Calais. Which seems to me an even better idea than sending it crashing into the sea!

The Guns Come to Bear

Although it was the RAF fighter pilots who were making the headlines in the first weeks of the battle against the flying bombs, the AA gunners on the ground were also playing their part, if in a less spectacular way. A report in *The Times* of Monday, 19 June endeavoured to give credit to both groups. 'There were indications last night', it read, 'that the combined efforts of the Anti-Aircraft guns and RAF fighters to bring down the pilotless aircraft over sea or in country districts are meeting with success.' And after describing how a Spitfire had shot down a V-1, the paper added: 'Shortly afterwards, AA gunners scored a success in the same locality. The tail unit of a pilotless aircraft was shot off and the machine dived straight down to blow up with a violent explosion.'

Unknown to the general public, however, the Anti-Aircraft Command, in particular its chief, General Sir Frederick Pile, had been having more than their fair share of problems in setting up their guns in the most effective positions as well as developing the best tactics against the fast-flying pilotless planes. In fact, it was not until 29 June that General Pile made his first public statement about the progress of the AA forces in trying to stop the V-1s.

'Some years ago,' he told a press conference, 'Lord Dowding, then the Chief of Fighter Command, expressed the view that if we could kill ten per cent in every German raid the pilots would be so upset that it would stop, and about twelve per cent of kills were achieved. Now we are faced with something completely different because we cannot frighten flying bombs. It is no use shooting down ten or twelve per cent of them – we must shoot down something like ninety per cent. The fighters and ourselves have put up our averages a good bit in the last few days, and although we have not yet got up to anywhere near the desired percentage of kills, I can say at the moment we are on the right road.'

Just how the AA got on the right road, why the guns were a while coming into action, and the manner in which the problems to counter the V-1 were overcome, are explained here by General Pile in an article written shortly after the events it describes had occurred.

The second Battle of Britain, the battle against the flying bomb, was as revolutionary in its scope and in its implications as had been those first engagements in World War I against the Taubes and Gothas which had led the attack of the heavier-than-air machine. Now we saw beginning the first battle of the robots. Human error was being gradually eliminated from the contest: in future, the machines would fight it out.

It was in the early hours of 13 June that I was awakened by an unusual certainty on the part of our local air-raid siren. There was an 'Alert' followed almost immediately by the 'All Clear', which, in turn, was followed almost at once by another 'Alert'. A few moments later my telephone rang in the darkness, and the Duty Intelligence Officer reported to me that Diver had at last arrived.

Seven flying bombs were plotted in this opening salvo, and one of them, followed by a discreetly observant Junkers 88, flew straight to London, where it crashed on to a railway viaduct at Bethnal Green, blocking all the lines out of Liverpool Street. This was a lucky beginning. The public were at first allowed to know nothing about it. They were told that an enemy aircraft had been shot down on to a railway bridge – indeed, it may be that we really did draw blood with the first shot of the new battle, for among the wreckage of the flying bomb was found a fuse of a heavy anti-aircraft shell. Three-quarters of an hour later another thirteen were plotted, and, after them, another two which seemed to have come from the Cherbourg Peninsula.

We reacted rather cautiously, in AA Command, to this new attack. We had been assured from above that we should have plenty of warning, perhaps as much as a month, before the enemy began to use his new weapon, and the general opinion was that these few salvoes of bombs were in the nature of a final gesture by the enemy, an attempt to test the possibilities of the flying bomb before the War was ended. And when, the next night, enemy activity reverted to normal, we were still uncertain whether to deploy the Diver defences. But the night after that, the night of June 15–16, sustained attacks began, and the battle was joined in earnest.

We had originally estimated that it would take us eighteen days to redeploy the defences against a flying-bomb attack, but this estimate had not gone unchallenged. Seven American AA battalions had been placed at our disposal, and five of them were still standing by awaiting orders to move. When we had said that the deployment would take eighteen days, although they were far from being fully mobile units, they had disagreed wholeheartedly. There would, they said, be insufficient early warning, and the whole movement would devolve into a chaotic last-minute scramble, the confusion of which they were not prepared to accept. So, while we stuck to our eighteen-day estimate, they planned an ambitious programme of moves that would fully redeploy them by the fourth day after the order was given. It turned out, of course, that even they had made an over-estimate. This initial deployment of 192 heavy anti-aircraft and the same number of light anti-aircraft guns was actually carried out in twenty-four hours – a remarkable feat when the implications of moving forty batteries of gunners with all their equipment and stores into new positions is considered.

By the end of June the deployment had swollen to 376 heavy guns and 576 40-mm equipments, in a belt stretching from Maidstone to East Grinstead, a total which did not include 560 light anti-aircraft weapons manned by the RAF Regiment along the South Coast. But numbers were by no means everything. Just at the beginning of the battle the London guns had joined in the shooting, but, unless they happened to blow up the flying bomb in the air, the mere act of hitting it was of little use, for all they succeeded in doing was to bring the missile down on to the very target at which it was aimed. It was thought preferable to leave the bombs alone, once they had reached the target area, in the pious hope that they would, as they sometimes did, pass on into the less densely populated countryside. For this reason the London guns were restricted from firing, and all that Londoners, who had got used to the comforting roar of the defences, saw was the flying bombs arriving and crashing and spreading devastation while all around there was a depressing silence.

There was no sign of any activity by the defences, and it was not long before the bitterly acid little tales reminiscent of those of the First World War, the early days of 1940, and, indeed, of any time when we failed to supply the answer quickly, began to be spread. It was said that the fighters were, of course, doing splendidly, but as for the guns – well, the less said about them the better.

As a matter of fact, there were very good security reasons why the gunners' contribution – which, I must confess, was not very impressive – could not be hinted at. We were not at all anxious for the enemy to find out what a strain had been put upon our resources, nor did we want it to be realised that the northern vulnerable areas now lay open and undefended against attack. But at the same time we were not getting the results we should have done. Here was a target which actually obeyed all the pre-war assumptions of anti-aircraft gunnery. It flew straight, at a constant speed and unchanging height. It should have been ideal. But our shooting was both wild and inaccurate. Many of the claims to have destroyed flying bombs arose from no more than the fact that the missile had reached the end of its course and, regardless of our fire, had dived to earth. At a generous estimate, I should think we were destroying perhaps 13 per cent of the targets.

There was something to be said on our side, however. The bomb, a very small target, flew at a high speed and at a height which was the most difficult of all to deal with: it was just too high for effective light anti-aircraft fire and too low for easy engagement by the heavy guns.

As early as February we had made it clear that we could only expect to destroy a very small percentage with our existing equipment. But, we said, if we could only get delivery of the equipment we had asked for from America, we should certainly do a lot better. In particular, we badly wanted the SCR 584, which provided with the electrical predictor a robot defence against the robot weapon. They had not yet been delivered, and we had to make do with what we had.

One thing we had been quite firm about was that there was a thousand-feet height-band, between 2000 and 3000 feet, where the effectiveness of anti-aircraft fire was likely to be small, and we were all greatly alarmed when this was just the height at which the majority of the flying bombs came in. There was no doubt about it that the enemy had thought everything out to the last detail. Even the routes along which the missiles were arriving seemed to be chosen for their awkwardness. There were other difficulties too. The low heights presented considerable problems to the radar sets, which had been sited, as far as possible, in hollows for technical reasons connected with the need for obtaining a natural screen against enemy interference or jamming. But no jamming was attempted, and the siting of the radar sets merely made it difficult, if not impossible, to pick up the targets until it was too late. This meant redeploying many of the batteries. Moreover, the scattering of 40-mm guns over the whole searchlight layout turned out to be an uneconomic proposition, so we decided we would redeploy them too. We selected new sites for them behind the heavy-gun belt in positions where, from the top of the North Downs, they would have a good field of fire. But, just as we had completed our reconnaissances, the Air Force decided to extend their balloon barrage to occupy the high ground which we had selected for our sites. This meant that we had to start all over again and choose some sites to the south of the heavy-gun belt. While we were doing this, we developed a means of using unseen fire-control methods by which the light guns might also engage the flying bombs under adverse weather conditions when fighters and the balloon barrage would become inoperable.

It was during this first stage of the battle that the ground and air defences were overlapping to such a degree that complicated rules for engagement of targets had to be laid down, giving priority now to one arm of the defences and now to the other according, mainly, to the state of the weather. Under certain conditions both fighters and guns operated together. These rules and the constant changing from one state to another, as well as the overlapping of spheres of influence, led to many opportunities being missed by one side or the other. The average fighter in those days had only a slight command of speed over the flying bomb, and required a large area in which to make its kill. As

84

things were, the fighter often had to break off the attack just as it was closing in, for no better reason than that it had reached the entrance to the gun zone. And as it was the fighters who were having the greater success (our percentage of kills had fallen to a figure as low as 9 per cent of the targets engaged), it was we who were almost invariably restricted. Never before had the guns been so forcibly restrained. Never before had the rules of defence been so complicated.

As was his habit whenever a crisis of any sort arose which might react on the war effort, Churchill took charge and held a series of conferences (on every second night). At these conferences he cross-examined us on what we were doing and what we were proposing.

I had been getting more and more frustrated by the continued restrictions on our freedom to engage the enemy. We had made immense efforts to get nearly 1000 guns into action. We had moved them on three occasions in order to comply with RAF modifications to the balloon layout. Now the procedure was so adverse to the guns that on many days they did not average five rounds apiece.

I had not failed to state our case at the various NAD meetings, and by the middle of July I was hardly on speaking terms with the other members. Once more I spoke as strongly as I could. I insisted that eventually the guns must be the answer, but that under present circumstances the guns never got a chance to improve. I further pointed out that the RAF, comparatively well as they had been doing, were still not really on terms with the menace and were not increasing their bag. As they had had a completely free run, it appeared as if other steps should be taken. The Prime Minister listened to what I and others had to say, and then said, 'All right, from next Monday for a week General Pile is to have a free hand.'

This was all very well, but I was not anxious to assume the major role in the defence until I had got more American equipment, and even then I wanted a combined show, in which the best results from the RAF as well as from the guns were obtained. Fortunately, events were moving fast, and when we did get that free run we had been demanding we had moved once more – this time to the South Coast – where conditions were much more favourable.

Very early in the battle we had discovered that the mobile 3.7-in gun, wonderful weapon though it was, was no match for the flying bomb. It could not be traversed smoothly enough at the high rates called for, and the results it gave were thus greatly inferior to those obtained by the static power-controlled guns. So we made up our minds that all AA Command mobile 3.7-in guns in the Diver defences should be replaced by the static power-controlled equipments. Looking back, it seems that this decision was, perhaps, of all the decisions we made during that time, the most vital. It really marked a turning-point in the struggle, and its adoption affected every stage of the battle.

Writing about it now, it looks a simple enough thing to do. But it caused the most fearful problems to arise and confront us. First, there was obviously no time in which to construct the standard holdfasts, which took months to complete even when one could get the labour to build them. This meant inventing and constructing a portable platform which could be fairly easily moved round with the equipment. My DDME, Brigadier Burls, devised a most ingenious affair, a movable lattice-work of steel rails and sleepers which, when filled with ballast, was as static as anybody could desire. Secondly, the power-controlled guns could only be obtained from operational sites in the less dangerously placed areas and had to be replaced in their turn by static hand-controlled guns. All of this meant a most complicated series of moves of heavy and unwieldy equipment not notably designed for ease of movement.

Consider the difficulties at a time when we were in the midst of a battle. Every redeployment of sites meant a complete reorganisation of the complicated signals circuits: for instance, the move forward of the light anti-aircraft guns meant that twelve new Gun Communication Rooms had to be provided for them, with all that that entailed. The changeover of the heavy anti-aircraft equipment meant that 441 static guns had to be uprooted and moved with all their stores, fire-control instruments, and so on from all over England to the Diver defences: 365 of them went by road, the remainder by rail. The portable platforms alone involved a move of 8000 tons of material. Special cranes were lent by the United States Army or provided by the War Office. Articulated tractors, too, were borrowed from the Americans, and the War Office found us some more transporters. Many of the gun-positions were without water: special RE Boring Section constructed wells and reservoirs. Roads of hard-core or Sommerfield track had to be laid down at marshy sites. Thirteen thousand Anderson shelters and three million sandbags were among the stores to be obtained. And just as the first thirty-two static heavy anti-aircraft guns had been installed, the balloon barrage extended its tentacles farther afield, and we had to find no fewer than a hundred new gun-sites. And just as we had completed this reconnaissance, another major development took place that undid, overnight, everything that we had already done.

In the plain, unadorned words of Mr Duncan Sandys, describing the affair afterwards: 'About the middle of July it was decided to take the bold step of moving the entire anti-aircraft belt down to the coast so that the guns should get an uninterrupted field of view.' Behind this simple description, a 'bold step' (a masterpiece of understatement in its way), there lay the story of a first-class row.

One of the difficulties of fighting a battle in England is that the Service Ministries find it almost impossible not to interfere. Heretofore Air Chief Marshal Sir Roderic Hill and I had moved guns and reported afterwards, and hardly had much exception been taken. But this 'bold' decision was tantamount to giving the guns priority over the fighters in the role of engaging the flying bomb.

The most tremendous beating of tom-toms took place. I think that it was considered in some important circles that Hill had been unduly influenced by myself, or by Sandys, or by both of us into agreeing to a move which would increase our successes and decrease the RAF's total. Which, of course, was just what it did do. The fact was that Hill, regarding the matter less parochially against the background of civilian death and destruction, realised, as we all did, that the Air Defence of Great Britain was a combined operation, that the combined efficiency of the defences was of greater importance than the individual glory of one or other Service, that what mattered was that, somehow, the flying bombs should be mastered, and it did not matter by whom. Anyway, the Air Council were very displeased. They left Hill in absolutely no doubt that he must take the full consequences of the failure – for failure was forecast in their every word – attending upon this decision. Much to everybody's surprise but our own, the move was the most enormous success, and Hill ended up on the Air Council.

The plan was that there should be a compact gun-belt all the way along the coast from Beachy Head to Dover, 5000 yards deep and firing 10,000 yards out to sea. This would give the fighters plenty of room for interception over the Channel and plenty of room for interception behind the guns, where they would be acting as wicket-keepers, with the balloons away in the distance as long-stops. Over the gun-belt the fighters would not fly below

The Evening News

NO. 19,464   LONDON, FRIDAY, JUNE 16, 1944   ONE PENNY

LATE EXTRA

OTLESS WARPLANES RAIDED BRITAIN

Morrison On Secret Weapon—and Counter Moves

'ACKS MAY ONTINUE

ht's raid on Southern England was by pilotless German aircraft, and re expected, announced Mr. Morrison of Commons to-day.

ting full reports of their effect, he warned to stay in the streets out of curiosity if our up in daylight. On the other hand, these ttacks need not be exaggerated.

ures are being applied with full vigour, and ual siren warning will continue.

Morrison's statement:

known for some time that the enemy was making the use of pilotless aircraft against this country, started to use this much-vaunted new weapon. A these weapons was used in the raids on Tuesday r fall was scattered over a wide area. A larger last night and this morning.

occasion the at- e caused a few se damage was inconsiderable. ack was more ve not yet full ll continue, and nce, the usual be given. Je. reparations have ised unnoticed. ares have been plied with full bable, however. g him where his rmation fded that it was ive the enemy n directing but g him where his fficult." he said. one from ordi- Therefore is here nformation pub- air raids in south of the line he Bristol Chan-

How to Spot Ghost Planes

1. **Great Speed**
2. **Bright Light**
3. **Smoke Trail**

DESCRIPTIONS of the German pilotless planes vary slightly in detail. But they agree on these points—terrific speed, bright lights, flames from exhaust, and very straight course.

One correspondent telephoned this picture of them to-day

"The planes have a distinctive, rhythmic note, giving the effect of a pulsating low throb. They are much smaller than a Spitfire, but have an appearance much the same.

"They are really midget planes. At night they show a distinct yellow glow at the rear, and in the light of searchlights streams of thick smoke can be seen being ejected from them.

"Many of them have been observed in daylight, and on several occasions R.A.F. fighters, with total disregard of the danger, have dived into the A.A. fire around them, in attempts to make a kill.

Brown or Black

"They appear to be painted a dark brown or black, the smoke issues from them in small thick puffs, attuned to the throb which can be heard

"They streak across the sky at a very great speed. They appeared to come across the Channel, and it is believed that at times two or three were sent over together."

The Home Security Ministry issued this advice to-day

When the engine of the pilotless aircraft stops and light at the end of the machine is seen to go out it may mean that the explosion will soon follow—perhaps in five to 15 seconds.

So take refuge from blast. Even those indoors should keep out of the way of blast and use the most solid protection immediately available.

OUR SCIENTISTS WILL DEFEAT IT

WHY WE BOMBED PAS DE CALAIS AREA

"Evening News" Reporter

IT should not be long before our war scientists and the R.A.F. take the full measure the German pilotless rocket bomber.

We have known for a long time that the enemy had this type of

[map of Normandy / Cherbourg peninsula]

FIVE-TONNERS HIT BOULOGNE E-BOAT PENS

R.A.F. DAY RAID

Air photographs taken after the great R.A.F. raid on Havre show no trace of E-boats or torpedo boats previously there. Reconnaissance pictures before the attack revealed ten E-boats and three torpedo boats.

THREE hundred R.A.F. heavies, escorted by Spitfires, attacked E-boat pens at Boulogne with 5,000-pounders before dark last night.

It was a replica of the blasting of Le Havre E-boat quays just 24 hours previously.

Lancasters and Halifaxes went to

Allied Striking Power Grows Steadily

CHERBOURG: THREAT INCREASING SUBSTANTIALLY

Six Miles to Cut the Escape Routes: Navy Shell Havre

The Navy have been shelling military targets and harbour installations at Havre, it was revealed at Supreme H.Q.

WITH our striking power growing steadily the Allied threat to the Cherbourg Peninsula is substantially increasing, it was stated to-day at Supreme H.Q.

American troops, writes the *Evening News*

EIGHTH LEAP
25 MILES

ADVANCE ALL ALONG LINE IN ITALY

ALLIED Armies in Italy have again advanced all along the front, says to-day's communique from General Alexander's H.Q.

"In the Adriatic sector, the enemy has withdrawn, and only slender contact has been maintained.

"Troops of the Eighth Army have captured Narni and Terni and advanced rapidly—more than 95 miles—taking Todi on the afternoon of June 15," adds the communique.

Key Traffic Centre

"To the West, other Eighth Army troops have advanced some 10 miles north of Orvieto.

"On their left troops of the Fifth Army have also advanced and have taken a number of towns, the most important of which is Acquapendente and leading elements are approaching Grosseto.

Terni, in the heart of Central Italy, is an important traffic and iron and steel centre, about 50 miles from Rome.

Narni is just south of Terni, both being on Highway Three.

Todi is midway between Terni and Perugia, which lies about 75 miles south-east of Florence.

Acquapendente is 65 miles north-west of Rome.

Bridges Hit

Detailing air operations to-day's communique says that "Medium bombers yesterday attacked a num.

bove: First news of the new German terror from the skies in June 1944.

low: A V-1 or 'Doodlebug', as the flying bombs became known, in flight.

Above: National newspaper cartoonists tri
to make light of the flying bomb menace:
'Oh, you're always thinking you can hear
flying bombs!' from the *Sunday Dispatch*,
22 June 1944.

Left: Cheers! No matter what the German
threw at the people of London they kept o
smiling – even in air raid shelters like this
one in Stoke Newington.

Below: The reality was actually
horrifying – one of the first V-1s to fall on
London was on 17 June at St John's Hill,
Clapham.

above: Artist's impression of an RAF fighter pilot attempting to shoot down a V-1 before it reaches
target.

below: Cross-section of a 'Doodlebug' from the *Aeroplane Spotter*, 29 June 1944.

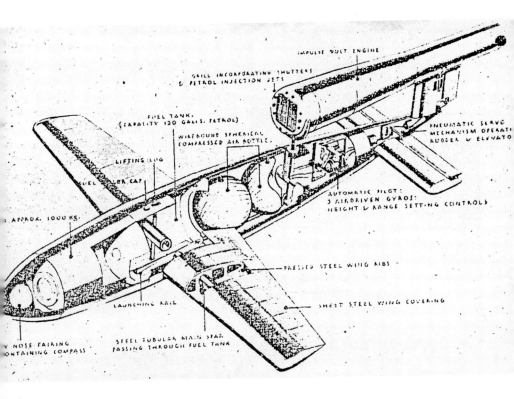

Right: One of the awesome V-2 rockets on a launching pad at Peenemunde.

Below: The noise of the V-1 rockets even became a source of fun for *Punch* cartoonists like Douglas Low in August 1944.

"I'm told that five seconds after the whirring sound stops it shouts a rude remark by Goebbels."

Below: A new and even more terrifying menace – the V-2 rockets – began to fall in September 1944. Croydon was destined to become 'Worst Bombed Borough' as this typical example in Hatch Road shows.

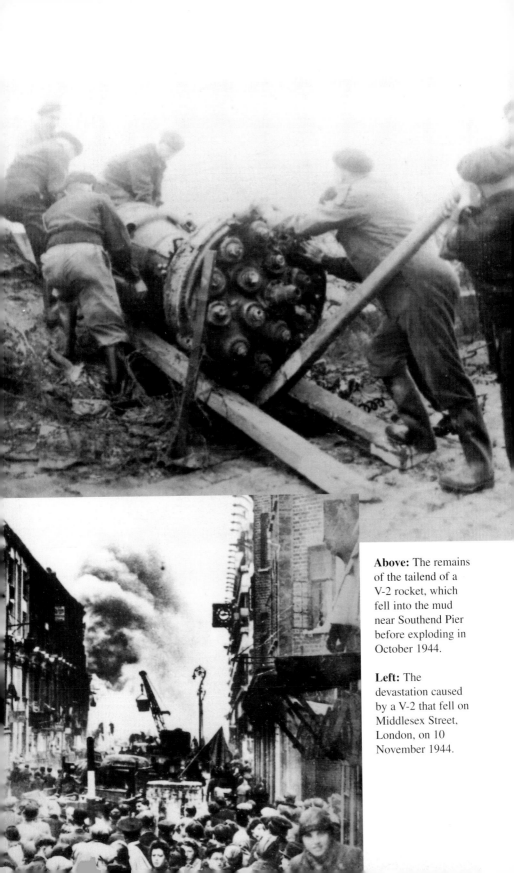

Above: The remains of the tailend of a V-2 rocket, which fell into the mud near Southend Pier before exploding in October 1944.

Left: The devastation caused by a V-2 that fell on Middlesex Street, London, on 10 November 1944.

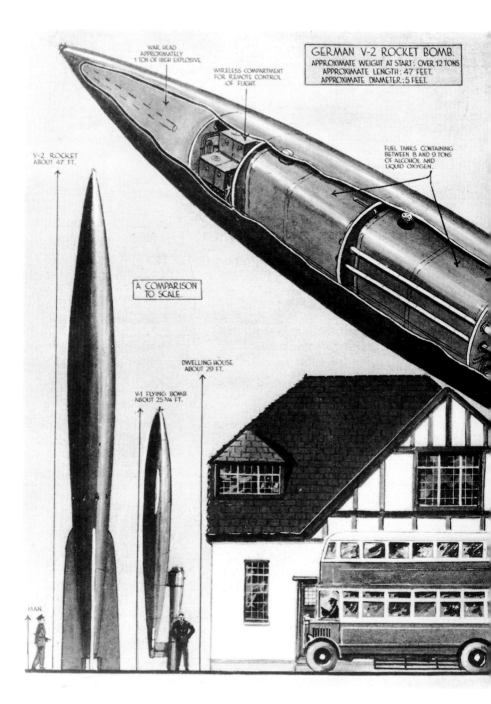

WAR HEAD
APPROXIMATELY
1 TON OF HIGH EXPLOSIVE.

WIRELESS COMPARTMENT
FOR REMOTE CONTROL
OF FLIGHT.

GERMAN V-2 ROCKET BOMB.
APPROXIMATE WEIGHT AT START: OVER 12 TONS
APPROXIMATE LENGTH: 47 FEET.
APPROXIMATE DIAMETER: 5 FEET.

FUEL TANKS CONTAINING
BETWEEN 8 AND 9 TONS
OF ALCOHOL AND
LIQUID OXYGEN.

V-2 ROCKET
ABOUT 47 FT.

A COMPARISON
TO SCALE.

DWELLING HOUSE
ABOUT 29 FT.

V-1 FLYING BOMB
ABOUT 25¾ FT.

MAN.

Another artist's impression of a cross-section of a V-2.

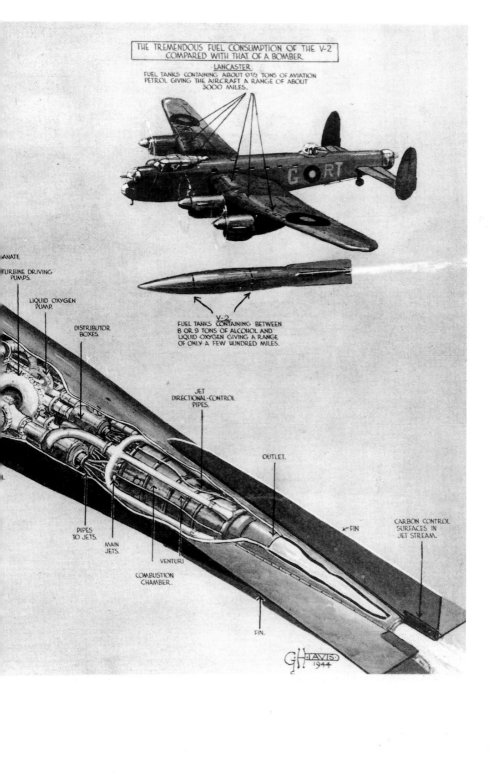

THE TREMENDOUS FUEL CONSUMPTION OF THE V-2
COMPARED WITH THAT OF A BOMBER

LANCASTER.
FUEL TANKS CONTAINING ABOUT 9½ TONS OF AVIATION
PETROL GIVING THE AIRCRAFT A RANGE OF ABOUT
3000 MILES.

V-2
FUEL TANKS CONTAINING BETWEEN
8 OR 9 TONS OF ALCOHOL AND
LIQUID-OXYGEN GIVING A RANGE
OF ONLY A FEW HUNDRED MILES.

ANATE
TURBINE DRIVING
PUMPS.

LIQUID OXYGEN
PUMP.

DISTRIBUTOR
BOXES.

JET
DIRECTIONAL-CONTROL
PIPES.

OUTLET.

PIPES
TO JETS.

MAIN
JETS.

VENTURI

COMBUSTION
CHAMBER.

←FIN

CARBON CONTROL
SURFACES IN
JET STREAM.

FIN.

G.H.DAVIS
1944

Left: American soldiers inspect a jet engine in a captured V-1 factory.

Below: After the end of the war the V-2 rocket became the first step in the conquest of space by American scientists at NASA.

Below left: A dramatic aerial photograph of the damage inflicted by Allied bombing raid on Peenemunde.

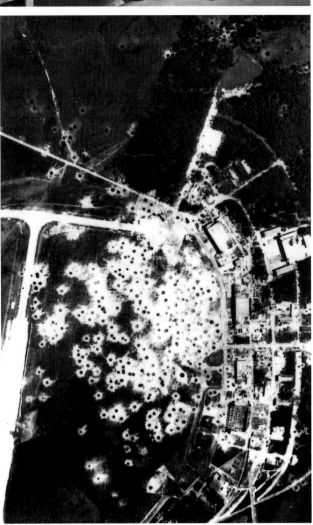

8000 feet, which allowed us absolute freedom up to 6000 feet. Another important factor was that there was much more hope of bringing flying bombs down harmlessly into the sea (if they were not exploded in the air) instead of bringing them crashing down on to the coastal towns. There had already been some unfortunate incidents arising out of good shooting.

The great trek southward began on 14 July. If we had thought that we were faced with a complex problem during our first development, with all the shuffling round that it caused us, what we had achieved then became very small game indeed compared with this emigration. For the initial redeployment 376 mobile heavy guns and 526 light guns had to be moved. The 32 static guns already emplaced had to be rooted up again and sent on their way, together with 70 more portable platforms which had arrived in the gun-belt. Forty static guns already en route had to be diverted to their new sites. The signals network, as complex an affair as can be imagined with its associated Gun and Searchlight Operation Rooms, had not only to be transferred, but to be ready in action before the guns arrived: inter-battery lines alone accounted for as much as 3000 miles of cable. While the move was in progress, the order had been given for the reinforcement of the defences by another 12 mixed heavy anti-aircraft batteries and 312 more static guns to equip all the Command heavy batteries with this type of weapon. Quite apart from the troops of the various supply services, 23,000 men and women had to be transported forward with all their kit and stores: 30,000 tons of stores of all sorts were lifted in one week by 8000 lorries and nearly 9000 RASC men. More than one million rounds of heavy anti-aircraft ammunition, weighing an additional 30,000 tons, were moved into the new defence belt. In this one week the vehicles of a supposedly static Command travelled 2,750,000 miles.

All the normal rules went by the board. Routing and movement control were forgotten. For this move one brigade issued no written orders at all: no one seemed any the worse. The movement was a flood, but a well-managed and orderly flood.

Moreover – and, looking back on it, the thing seems almost unbelievable – the move of the heavy guns to the coast which had begun on 14 July was completed in three days. By dawn, on 17 July, the heavies were in action again. Two days later, only five days from the word 'Go', the light guns, which had remained behind to cover the moves of the heavies, were also in action.

It was an extraordinary achievement, particularly as this was not the only deployment upon which we were engaged. At the same time as the southward move was taking place, another move was in progress towards the east.

For some time there had been evidence of a minor threat, a diversionary attack in the flying-bomb battle. It appeared that, by one means or another, the enemy was launching flying bombs in such a manner that they also came up the Thames estuary. A 'box' defence, north and south of the river, was hastily reconnoitred and 208 heavy anti-aircraft guns and nearly 450 light guns of both 40-mm and 20-mm calibre were deployed. Another 144 heavies were held in reserve in case they should be wanted, and we were ready to reinforce the Maunsell forts with improvised defences sited on sunken barges. The staff, already fully occupied with these two deployments, were faced with all the problems attendant upon an improvised sea-going defence. There were such nautical matters as the state of the tides to be considered. The provision of reliefs and ammunition, of power supplies and rations by water, were new variations on familiar themes.

It was extremely fortunate that our AA Command staffs were, as was generally admitted, of a very high standard indeed: no Commander was better served than I by his back-room boys.

As if these deployments were insufficient to keep us out of mischief, it was at this moment – at this critical stage in the second Battle of London – that we were asked to consider how we might contribute another 25,000 men from our dwindling supply of manpower. It was lucky that the capture of the Cherbourg Peninsula had automatically led to the cancellation of the Bristol Diver defences. This released a certain number of men, but the rest had still to be found from the searchlight troops and smoke companies.

But, in spite of all our problems and all our difficulties, from that moment the tide of the battle turned. From that moment the scale of success increased steadily and without question.

The man in charge of the Balloon Barrage to which General Pile referred was Air Vice Marshal W C Gell, and he, too, presented a short report on the achievements of his men and their 'monstrous silver jumbos' at a press conference on 7 September 1944. At its full extent, the barrage stretched from Redhill to Chatham and covered 260 square miles, creating an unforgettable and rather beautiful sight in the skies over the North Downs of England. With typical British humour, the Air Vice Marshal liked to refer to his balloons as the 'Goalkeepers of London'.

The Balloon Barrage was the final defence line against the flying bombs which had escaped the fighters and guns. When the first curtain of 500 balloons was decided upon, I very quickly found that it was required outside the normal London barrage area where no previous facilities for this type of defence existed.

A reconnaissance party was at once sent forth to stake out the sites, and some of these were in such remote spots that it was even necessary to build roads capable of carrying the heavy lorries transporting hydrogen cylinders and other equipment and supplies.

It was on 16 June that Balloon Command HQ received a signal ordering the deployment of the barrage and no sooner were these 500 balloons in position and flying than another 500 were ordered. This meant finding and preparing more sites, and one squadron travelled 300 miles with all its equipment to answer the call from the south.

But even before the second 500 were in position, a third order was received increasing the total to 1,750, making this the greatest concentration of balloons ever assembled. Squadrons were rushed south from all over Britain; five thousand miles of telephone cable were laid by GPO engineers, RAF Signals and the Royal Corps of Signals to connect all the sites to head-quarters; and WAAF telephonists were brought in to man the instruments.

To transport personnel and supplies including hydrogen cylinders from factories to all parts of the country, a fleet of some 3,000 vehicles was assembled. Their drivers worked a 24-hour system and many of them did not remove their clothes for days on end!

Like the fighter-pilots and AA gunners, the balloon crews kept unbroken vigil, snatching brief periods of sleep whenever there was a lull. Many of them were in the front line again for the first time since the Blitz and had the perilous satisfaction of seeing many a flying bomb brought down by the cables of their balloons or deflected from their course. To catch their victims the balloons were generally flown at heights between 1,000 and 5,000 feet, depending on their proximity to London.

Sometimes the robot would explode in the air after striking the cable; but more often, spitting furiously and wiggling its tail from side to side like a fish, it crashed on or near the balloon site or an adjacent searchlight battery, and, needless to say, there were casualties. Five sites received direct hits from the flying bombs they had netted although the crews had already taken the precaution of going to ground.

Each impact necessitated at least one new balloon and hydrogen to inflate it as well as a new cable to attach to it. But on the plus side we accounted for 278 V-1s which had escaped the fighters or guns.

Even as grim an affair as the fight against the flying bomb can have its humorous moments and one story – and I shall not say if it concerned the guns or the balloons – is worth repeating. There is, of course, a healthy rivalry among the individual crews manning the ground defences in claiming credit for every doodlebug destroyed.

One day, however, a V-1 whose flight towards London was successfully interrupted was ill mannered enough to plunge into the camp and write off the tent and personal belongings of no less a person than the Commanding Officer. And believe it or not, none of the crews seemed anxious to claim it!

Life in Doodlebug Alley

By 19 July, General Pile's 'gun belt' had 412 heavy guns, 1,184 light guns and 200 rocket barrels in position across a swathe of southern England to repel the flying bombs. And thanks to the combined operations of the AA and Fighter Command, in a week-long period which followed only 200 of the 473 V-1s fired at England reached the Greater London area. But statistics do not tell the story of what life was like for the ordinary folk of southern England trying to carry on with their everyday lives under the shadow of this onslaught. One man who knew the area of Kent, Sussex and Surrey over which the majority of the flying bombs appeared on their way towards London was H E Bates, the author of that classic novel of country life, *The Darling Buds of May*. Bates was then a serving squadron leader in the RAF as well as being the Air Ministry's 'writer in residence'. 'Apart from contributing factual articles about the service to various journals and magazines in Britain and America, he also wrote a series of popular short stories about the lives of RAF personnel in wartime which were published under the pseudonym 'Flying Officer X'.

During the course of the flying-bomb attacks on England, Bates was asked by the Air Ministry to keep notes on the attacks in preparation for a booklet which, it was hoped, would commemorate this period of the hostilities in much the same way as an earlier publication, *The Battle of Britain*, by Hilary St George Saunders, had done. Bates, for his part, completed the task early in 1945, but due it seems to inter-departmental wrangling about just who should take the credit for defeating the V-1, the booklet was never published and has remained on file ever since. Published here for the first time is the section of Bates' report which deals most graphically with those who felt the greatest impact of the German weapon. No item written in hindsight that I have read has been able to evoke with such feeling and immediacy the events recorded here.

In south-eastern England life in the summer of 1944 rapidly became something of a nightmare. If in America the doodlebug remained for some time a subject for cartoons and in the rest of England little more than the subject of a stereotyped communique, it was because hardly anyone there *knew* what the doodlebug looked like or sounded like or what a man's emotions were as he heard and watched an entirely robot aeroplane roaring like a harsh and hideous express train across the sky. And a man's emotions were not pleasant.

The doodlebug could be heard from a long way off. It came out of the clear summer distance or out of the rain or the dark July cloud with a low level roar that could be heard about thirty miles away. It seemed to fly on an invisible track, as straight as a train. As it came nearer the roar became a metallic throb like the fiery stroke of a cheap motor-bike, and as it passed overhead these throbs set up the most deafening reverberations that were like the explosion of a continuous back-fire.

And since the enemy's favourite tactics were to launch the bombs in salvoes, they rarely came singly. As many as half a dozen would come roaring over together on parallel tracks separated by about a mile. The noise was fantastic. Crows in the fields rose up with their own terrified explosion of wings and in houses dogs and cats cowered in their own secret places for shelter.

95

People who had never been frightened by the sound of a bomb or a bomber found themselves nervous at the roar of the doodlebug.

But if the noise of its travelling was bad enough, its sudden silence was worse. That sudden silence meant that somewhere, sooner or later, the bomb was coming down. Sometimes a bomb was hit by guns or fighters over the coast and floated silently inland for some miles before falling. Sometimes it tilted into a steep dive and went straight to earth. Sometimes the engine in the gyroscopic control did not seem to be working normally and the bomb came along slower, coughing and missing its strokes and picking them up again, or sailing crazily round the countryside on what seemed to be an elliptical course. Frequently, and in fact very frequently from the middle of July, it appeared with as many as half a dozen fighters in pursuit, rather like so many young dogs chasing an electric hare.

The golden wink of their guns in the wings could be seen a few seconds before the sound of them could be heard. If you were directly below them it was a moment of tense and terrifying beauty. For the impact of the shells on the bomb came at about the same moment as the shells being fired, and in the few seconds of interval you could only wait with breathless and uncertain excitement. If there was no impact and the bomb was not hit you knew that it would fly on until the fighter attacked it again and you knew, not without a certain natural human relief, that for the moment you were safe again. But you knew, too, that it would go on until it was forced down or came down of its own accord, and that wherever it came down the lives of innocent and decent people would be terrorised or blown into a thousand unrecognisable pieces.

If, on the other hand, the bomb was hit and the fighters turned suddenly and steeply away you had two chances. There was a chance, and it was a good chance, that the bomb would burst in the air, exploding into countless pieces that did nothing more than frighten the birds, the blast of it simply absorbed by the spaces of sky. Or there was a chance that if it came down the bomb would fall harmlessly in woods or fields, hurting nothing but a sheep or two. And since the English countryside is not so thickly populated as statisticians sometimes seek to show, that was a good chance, too.

All this happened by day; and it happened also, with some differences, at night. By day the people of Kent and Sussex could stop their work in hayfields or cherry-orchard or shop or factory, or wherever it was and calculate the behaviour of the bomb by what they could see and hear. But at night it was rather different. Every night the authorities sounded an air-raid warning as darkness fell, whether in fact bombs were approaching or not. In this way the population of London and the south-east was told that they were expected to try to rest if they could. And very sensibly the greater part of the population went to bed. But if you lived in that part of the countryside that became known as 'Doodlebug Alley' going to bed was a curious experience. When bombs came you had, as in the day time, two chances. You could get out of bed and into shelter; or you could stay in bed and hope. Hoping, curiously enough, was the chance that thousands and thousands of sturdy English country citizens took every night for about eighty nights in the summer. They lay in bed and listened to the bombs travelling up on their courses from the coast; they listened to the sound of night-fighters firing; and they listened, too, for the worst sound of all: the sound of silence. And in that miserable, taut, uncertain existence they were very brave.

The people of 'Doodlebug Alley' were in fact never free. In eighty days and nights they had every chance to see and hear practically everything a flying bomb could do. They saw it fall on their ancient and beloved

97

churches, on schools and hospitals, on some of the loveliest villages not only in England but the world. They saw the monuments and landmarks of centuries go down in dust. They never knew from one moment to another whether the meal they were eating, the glass of beer they were drinking, or the dart they held poised in their hand ready to throw at the saloon-bar board might not be their last. They said goodbye to their children as they went to school in the morning and never knew if they would see them again.

The Battle of Britain, which they had been thrilled and proud to see with their own eyes in the glorious summer days of 1940, was a memory without fear. The Battle of the Doodlebug, if ever they thought of it like that, was a time entirely without thrill or pride. They hated it; the edges of their nerves were rubbed raw by it; and they saw in it, beyond their taut day-to-day, meal-to-meal existence, all its hideous potentiality for the future. All this was hidden behind the flat face of those drab communiqués which security and war impose on us. Behind the words 'flying bombs were again launched against southern England; damage and casualties have been reported' there lay and indeed still lie a million unrecorded thoughts not so much about what the doodlebug did to the world of England in 1944 as the world of the future it foreshadowed for us all.

If the country citizen in Kent and Sussex lived through the summer in a state of tautness and grim anger, justified by his own phlegmatic English courage, he knew that he had always, wherever he was, two chances. They were terribly simple. The flying bomb would either fall or fly on. And since in plain fact the bomb was not meant for him, his second chance was very good. But in London the citizen had only one chance. He knew there that the bomb must fall. He knew quite well that it was intended for him. The target was not the matchless countryside of Kent and Sussex, but the vast and congested area of London.

In Scotland Yard, the modest red and white building of Whitehall, mythically represented by thousands of detective writers and gravely viewed every day by thousands of American soldier sightseers, there hangs a map of the Metropolitan Police area of London. It represents the largest urban-human target in the world. Twenty miles across, covering 95 boroughs, living space of eight million people, home of historic monuments and churches and every kind of building from the Dickensian slums of the east to the garden suburbs of the north-west and the palaces of Kings; huge, congested, monstrous, unmistakable, a target that cannot be missed. Its very enormity allows the greatest margin of inaccuracy.

If you aim at the docks and hit the Guildhall, if you aim at Victoria Station and hit the Tower of London, if you aim at Battersea Power Station and hit the house where Dickens wrote *Pickwick*, it does not really matter. You are always very near the bull's eye. You never miss. The impossible immensity of London together with its geographical position in relation to the Continent creates for it dangers unknown in the same degree by any other city in the world. To the aimers of the flying bombs London was the perfect target. They knew that an error of as much as twenty miles still gave them a score.

It was therefore very natural that on the afternoon of 3 August Mr Churchill, giving to a crowded House of Commons a report of the first seven weeks of flying-bomb war, should have spoken at once of 'famous and mighty London'. He knew quite well that London is not only the greatest material target but the greatest propaganda target in the world. He knew also, as the following words show, that the Germans placed that propaganda value first and its material value second.

99

'If the Germans imagine that the continuance of this present attack, which has cost them very dear in every branch of production,will have the slightest effect upon the course of the war or upon the resolve of the nation or upon the morale of the men, women and children under fire they will only be making another of those psychological blunders for which they have so long been celebrated... There is no question of diverting our strength from the extreme prosecution of the war, or of allowing this particular infliction to weaken in any way our energetic support of our Allies.'

Nevertheless Mr Churchill knew, and now quite frankly stated, that the material cost of those first seven weeks was very great. He had the painful job of announcing, in figures that were a shock to the rest of England and the outside world, exactly what had been happening to what had been known as Southern England.

In seven weeks 5,340 flying bombs had been launched, or more than 100 per day; 4,735 persons had been killed, with 14,000 more or less seriously injured. There had been many slightly injured. It was 'a sad tale of human sorrow and suffering'. Yet looked at in the least distressing way, it meant that each bomb launched had killed on an average one person. But if the bomb was not so costly in life as had been feared, it was very costly in property. It was terrifying in its surface blast. In seven weeks it had totally destroyed 17,000 houses and had damaged 800,000 more. By blasting windows and roofs over a tremendous area it had made thousands homeless. It had split families, disorganised social life; had driven out of London about 1,000,000 people who had no war business there.

At the same time, with that curious disregard for danger which is part of the inexplicable essence of living, about the same number of people appeared to be coming back to London as were leaving it. Foolhardy though it might have been, as Mr Churchill pointed out, that fact gave 'the lie in most effective measure to the fantastic German stories of London being in panic under the perpetual pall of smoke and flame.'

Nevertheless flying-bomb horrors were very many and very real; and Mr Churchill could offer no hope that they would end. On that day, 3 August, the Allied line in Normandy ran from Avranches to Caen; the greater part of the flying-bomb bases were a hundred miles to the east. Until they were captured the flying bomb menace could not end. Nor, in all probability, would it end then. It was known that flying bombs could be launched from carrier aircraft and it was known also that the flying bomb, which the Germans liked to call V-1, was likely sooner or later to be replaced or supplemented by V-2. That weapon, of which Mr Churchill had warned the House in February, would in all probability be a stratospheric rocket of greater range, greater power and even greater inaccuracy than the first. It might even be followed by another, V-3 and even, if you were to believe the propaganda threats by Dr Goebbels, by V-4. Whatever those weapons were and however they might come, they were intended, as Mr Churchill said, 'to produce a great deal more mischief'.

The Churchilian statement of that afternoon of 3 August was necessarily general and incomplete. It could only hint at the vast organisations behind the scenes; the long-prepared plans for Civil Defence, National Fire Service, Health Service, Police Services, hospitals, railways, buses, shelters, feeding centres, evacuation, building repairs, emergency housing and the care of young and aged and sick. It could only hint at the state of morale and whether, if it was high or low, it had changed since the Blitz of 1940. It could only touch on the broad grey lines and not the thin bitter personal etchings of trial and suffering. It could say nothing of the sharp humour, the dry resignation, the incongruous comedies of the first seven weeks of the new menace to civilised living.

In point of fact much had been done. Much had changed. All the vast organisations which are the foundation of morale in times of crisis – hospitals, Civil Defence, Fire Services and so on – had changed their methods as their experience grew. All of them had been warned of the possible coming of the flying bomb; all of them had made arrangements to meet it. Yet none of them knew what a flying bomb would do when it came and most of all what it would do to morale. In reality it did a great deal to morale. Its effects were in some ways violently different from the effect of the Blitz of 1940. In that year the bomb had driven people closer together; it had drawn them closer into communities for shelter, feeding, clothing, friendliness and comfort. In 1944 the flying bomb seemed to drive them apart. In 1940 there were few personal shelters; a vast population slept in the Tubes. In 1944 tens of thousands of houses in London had their personal shelters, some of Anderson type outside or Morrison type inside, others of the reinforced basement type under the house. There were also great numbers of street shelters. To all these, which were part of the street or the house, the people tended to cling with that peculiar tenacity of pride and affection which makes the Englishman's home his castle.

No longer, in fact, did the citizen tend to leave his home when the bomb menaced it or the bomb fell. He clung to it instead. That admirable organisation, the Women's Voluntary Service, noted in the course of its tireless and wonderful work all over the bombed areas that it was no longer easy to bring bombed citizens to feeding centres. Food had to be taken to the people. Kerbside feeding replaced communal feeding. More and more people refused to leave their bombed homes. They worked frantically in the chaos.

The police of the much-bombed district of Croydon noted the same thing. Women were found dusting with scrupulous care the window sills of blasted houses, excusing themselves with 'Must make it look a bit decent, you know' – expressing that pride of street and house which is more than self-respect. This same intense desire to hold on to normal life was seen also in the crazy behaviour of a young man who insisted, against all threats and advice, on going back into a house that was about to collapse. 'Knock 'im down, guv'nor, I can't do nuthin' with 'im', said his father to the policeman, 'knock 'im down afore he does 'isself any 'arm.' The young man exhibited terrific anxiety to fight anyone who laid hands on him. 'And what,' said the policeman, 'do you want to go into the house for?' The young man grew very excited. 'You see, guv'nor, I'm being married this morning and all me money's in the 'ouse and I gotta get it somehow.' So the policeman gave permission for the boy to go into the house; at which there was no longer any controlling his father. 'Blimey, guv'nor, if he's goin' in I'm goin' in! I gotta pair o' boots in there.'

To this category also belongs the lady with the black leather bag. She is a spiritual sister to the old lady who said, 'They ain't human', and to the other old lady who said, 'Ain't they sly?' She is one with the thousand ladies all over London who have been carrying their black bags to the shelters every night for five years and whose constant watchword has been, 'Damn Hitler. Where's my Guinness?' As this old lady crawled out from under the debris of her smashed house, shaken, covered with dust, bruised, she thought only of her black leather bag. 'Is me bag all right?' she said. 'Yes,' they said, the bag was all right. Was there something important in it? 'I'll say it's important,' she said, 'it's me bottle of whisky.' In that case, they suggested, this was probably a good time for her to take a drop. 'Not on your life,' the old lady said. 'I'm saving that for an emergency.'

The woman dusting the window-ledge where there is no longer any window, the young man fighting to rescue his marriage money, the old ladies clinging, through their symbolic black bags, to a life that even in its extremes of terror never becomes a 'time of emergency': all these are part of the story of London morale. But they are not the whole story. Morale is not compounded of tangible experience. It is something in the air.

And the something that was in the London air of Summer 1944 was very different from the something that was in the air in Winter 1940. Morale had not fallen; it had simply grown thinner. People were distracted and bewildered rather than very afraid. When courage has to be spread over twenty-four hours of the day it grows thin towards the end of them. The Londoner has always shown a singular tenacity about his city. Now both the WVS and the police noted that this tenacity had become more personal. Londoners began to cling to their own bits of London, shattered or whole, and something pathetic and wonderful was to be seen in their bewildered devotion to shapeless scraps of what had once been home. The scraps were sometimes not even shapeless. The doodlebug in the space of a clouded split-second blew the mansion, the hospital, the cottage, the top floor back room into a tower of dark dust that settled into something indistinguishable from the dust of a Nineveh and Pompeii. The bomb-ruin is not only international but timeless, too.

The WVS, tireless, superbly efficient, infinitely adaptable, fed this thinned morale from mobile canteens, cars, even hand-carts. It distributed hot meals, tea, chewing gum from America, gallons of chocolate. It helped to evacuate from the city 307,768 mothers, in 500 special trains. It sent 3,000 of its members with them, and with the members 7,000 urns of tea.

In one week of July it evacuated 1,448 expectant mothers. It provided 200,000 garments for people who had lost everything but the things they stood up in. It provided in one day 576 babies' bottles and 1,152 teats.

It evacuated children under 5 and, most difficult of all, people of over 65. Its organisation, in which the la-di-da milady worked side by side with the cockney street warden, was everywhere, at all times, night and day, wherever bombs were coming down.

They earned for themselves that rarest of all tributes: the tribute given by the North to the South. It came from a Lancashire man sent to London on bomb-damage reconstruction. He had never seen or heard a bomb in his life; he was a man to whom, as to thousands of others, a siren sounding an alert was a fearful event and who, as the flying bombs began to fall, promptly took up his bed and dived into the nearest and deepest shelter. He was arrested in his flight by the sight of WVS drivers, not all of them young, but all of them certainly tired, calmly going out on duty into a concentration of doodlebugs. His courage came back. Next day he was heard to say, in a classic sentence which it is to be hoped the censor will tolerate since those of whom it was made are very proud of it: 'See them? Them's best bloody bitches in t'world.'

Figures tell something, but not all. The Lancashire man with his crisp and coloured tribute says more for an army of women than all its own impressive figures of work and succour can ever do. So with the damaged home. Figures will tell you that a single flying bomb causes damage within an area of 20 or 30 acres, demolishes beyond repair 20 or 30 houses, slightly damages 400–1,000 others. Yet the picture of an old lady on the train going north, holding the canary in its cage in one hand and her grandson in the other, and in her glassy, flabby eyes a look of 'So this, after all, is what we have come to', tells of something that is too deep for tears.

In the same way the miles and miles of anonymous blasted roofs all across south and south-east London meet the eye and only succeed, after a time, in tiring it. The real picture only comes alive at the sight of thousands and thousands of hay-rick tarpaulins, bright green and grey and brown, sent from farmers and builders all over the country, spread over the tileless roofs of the city.

The heap of rubble that was a London home never had any meaning for us, the outside world. But the heap of rubble that was the Guards' Chapel at Buckingham Gate in London meant something to us all. On a fine Sunday summer morning, as the dahlias were coming into bloom beyond the plane trees in the park across the road, a whole congregation of serving soldiers, men and women, were lost with the chapel in which they worshipped. From that time onward, an average of one historic building of one sort or another was damaged or destroyed in London every day. In Holborn the lovely Staple Inn, in Westminster St George's Church, in Kensington Holland House, in Fulham the Palace, in Hammersmith the Friends' Meeting House, in the City of London Customs House and five churches and many others, in Greenwich Charlton House, in Camberwell Dulwich College, in Southwark the Cathedral – day after day London added another name to its already long list of damaged historic treasure.

The flying bomb, as we have seen, could never miss. It fell in the gardens of the poor and in the gardens of Buckingham Palace. And it fell, mostly south of the Thames, in those tightly congested boroughs that were the nineteenth century's contribution to town planning. Into these miles and miles of streets, from the mean desolation of the river-side wharf alleys made more desolate by the bombing of 1940, to the lighter outer suburbias of Croydon and Penge, the flying bombs poured in on their fixed routes with shocking reiteration. The theory that no two bombs ever fall in the same place was disproved again and again. Robot design and robot power made it certain that they would often do so. Flying in from the south-east they made landfall again and again just short of the city's centre. The boroughs of Croydon, Penge, Beckenham, Dulwich, Streatham and Lewisham were under the severest sort of bombardment day after day.

The little Victorian borough of Penge, tiny beside the huge area of neighbouring Croydon, claims to have suffered more, for its size, than any other area in London. Penge at least will show what can happen to a single congested area. Penge is a mile square, its post-Victorian façade has a look of substance since proved to be false. It has 6,000 houses. Yet in 80 days it had 10,000 houses damaged. This odd statement is explicable by the fact that some thousands of houses were damaged a second time. And after evacuation 1 in 20 of the remaining population was killed or injured. The rest had literally no roof over their heads.

Let Penge then, with a few general figures, finish off the picture of all the south and south-eastern area of metropolitan London as it looked by the middle of August. And let the builders – whose job in this blitz made the job of practically any other service look by comparison quite small – supply the figures. By the end of July production of window-covering materials had increased to a million yards a week. Each week two million tiles and two million slates were brought to London. Of those picturesque hayrick covers already mentioned there were 150,000 in use, together with unnumbered thousands of ladders, at one time. And in addition, there arrived or were calculated as being necessary in the long future of reconstruction: 150,000,000 tiles or slates; 200,000,000 square feet of ceiling and wallboard; 50,000,000 square feet of glass; 400,000 doors; 340,000 lavatory basins; 50,000 sinks; 50,000 WC cisterns; 70,000 WC pans; and 50,000 water storage tanks.

To all these demands for the very fundamental necessities of human living were added demands for furniture, crockery, bedding – all the things, officially known as goods and chattels, that make up home. Much furniture was salvageable. This in itself created a big problem of removal and storage. Let Croydon and Wandsworth supply the figures this time. In Wandsworth 125 bombs made necessary no less than 7,000 removals, of which 4,200 went to store. In Croydon 137 bombs made 3,000 removals necessary, of which exactly half went to store. All this was repeated in twenty other boroughs. Soldiers, RAF, American forces, council workers and contractors all helped in fact to salvage enough furniture for no less than 50,000 removals.

H E Bates' account of life in 'Doodlebug Alley' makes a particular point of the role of women in the battle against the V-1. This theme was also highlighted by another writer, Vivien Batchelor, who told the story of one remarkable London wife and mother in a piece for the *Evening Standard* of 8 September.

The women of London were perhaps the bravest of all as they carried out their ordinary household tasks, standing in queues for that little extra something to keep up the family morale, falling flat on their faces if a flying bomb cut out over them, but getting up and carrying on again unshaken.

Mrs Janet Blagg, born and brought up in London's East End, was one of these. During one night a flying bomb fell in her street and demolished half of her six-roomed house. But it left the kitchen intact and Mrs Blagg was expecting her husband, a heavy rescue worker, home from all-night duty.

Although she was badly cut and shaken, she took her shopping bag and stood in line at the fish shop, just as the sirens went again. As she stood in the queue a bomb came over. Its engine cut and all the women heard the devilish scream as it dived towards them.

108

Down went the housewives, covering their heads with their baskets. Flying glass was a thing they had learned to avoid in London. Down came the bomb and some of the women never rose again. Their little packages were strewn all over the road, their clothes were torn and their shoes blown off, but they were past caring.

Mrs Blagg was lucky. For the second time in six hours she escaped with just some more cuts. The fish shop had only minor damage and the fish was stored in refrigerators.

'I got a bit of haddock,' she said later, 'and I got back to what was left of our place just as my old man came in. He'd been tunnelling under a block of flats to rescue a woman and her baby. Alive they were. He was that hungry, too.'

Without a word, Mrs Blagg set about getting her husband his well-earned meal. And of her own double escape from death she said not a word.

America and the
Flying Bomb

H E Bates mentioned that although US servicemen were
involved in the war, the American people knew little at first
about the dangers that England was facing from the V-1. It
was thanks mainly to two American war correspondents
that this was changed: a broadcaster named Raymond
Gram Swing, and the famous novelist Ernest Hemingway.
While Swing used several of his daily broadcasts in the
summer of 1944 to acquaint his listeners with the flying
bomb, Hemingway wrote a magazine piece about the RAF's
battle with the V-1s which was subsequently described as a
'masterpiece of war reporting'. Here, first, is Raymond
Gram Swing's report, 'America and the Flying Bomb',
which was heard by listeners on both sides of the Atlantic
on Friday, 7 July. Apart from its insight into the reasons for
the secrecy surrounding the raids, it is also remarkably
prophetic about the potential of the flying bomb after the
war is over.

London, once more, is a central point in the concern and
sympathy of the people of the United States. Prime
Minister Churchill's revelations as to the seriousness of
the robot bombs took this country aback. We had not
realised what London was experiencing. The hints
which passed through the censorship had not whipped
up our imaginations. We had no inkling that the German

secret weapon was formidable, or that the British leaders had been preoccupied with it for so many months, or that the danger from it when it finally appeared was much different from that of the Big Berthas which shelled Paris in the last war. London under the blitz was close to the hearts of people in this country, and the city's sufferings created more of the reality of fellowship than a dozen successful political conferences. Some of that sense of fellowship passed as London's ordeal ended. Now much of it has been suddenly renewed. And it is all the more vivid for the fact that many Americans are in London and are sharing their full part of the dangers and the work of rescue.

Mr Churchill's speech made a further contribution to American regard for the British. He told the truth; told it fully and freely, and told it without a moment's bitter fulmination, a restraint that was unique in the circumstances. He did not seem to hold back anything that required telling with an appeal to that vastly elastic word 'security'. And he did not slip the truth in as fragments here and there in a tirade of passion. There was a dignity about Mr Churchill's performance to be achieved only in a free community, and this fact registered in this country. That the British should cry out for reprisals is well understood; that the robot bombs have dissipated any chance, if there was such a chance, for a spirit of conciliation, also was appreciated. *The New York Times* today remarks that Germany has forfeited the right to complain about anything the world inflicts on her in retribution and atonement. The robot bombs have not only influenced the mood of the peace but some thoughts about the actual peace terms themselves. It suddenly is realised that the robot bombs are in their infancy and can mature into something with which the world must be concerned through a long future. A disarmed nation can make these bombs. It can make them without possessing an air force, a navy or an

111

army. A few ardent scientists working in a secluded factory compose a peril to a peaceful neighbour, and a peril so great that, as now, the concentrated force of military, air and naval power cannot cope with it. The permanent supervision of German industry in the post-war world would seem to be now settled. But that is not all of the problem. In organising the peace after this war, how is industry to be supervised in any other country where a small conspiracy of inventors and industrialists might set out to terrorise a neighbour? Here is a problem in prevention that will be as difficult to solve as the immediate problem of mitigating the offence of the robot bombs on London. These mechanical demons have not only changed the nature of this war, but concepts about the very nature of organised peace itself.

Coincidental with this report, the first American victims of a flying-bomb attack were reported – although one of the men involved in the direct hit, a Sergeant Ed Bearefoot, had a remarkable escape from death as this account from the *Daily Mail* of 9 July reveals:

AMERICAN SERGEANT BURIED ALIVE
FOR THREE DAYS

An American Army sergeant was entombed for three and a half days beneath the piled wreckage of his billet in southern England, which was shattered by a flying bomb, before he was rescued.

Sergeant Ed Bearefoot was in a room with two other United States soldiers when the flying bomb dropped and the place fell about them. He was thrown to the floor and the beams collapsed, but somehow stayed fixed above him. Even the great weight of debris crashing down on top of the beams did not dislodge them.

Debris was removed piece by piece by rescuers, and when they finally lifted Sgt Bearefoot out unharmed, but dazed, covered in dust, very thirsty and very hungry, he had been in prison for eighty-five and a half hours. He was taken to hospital where he is said to be rapidly recovering.

The bodies of his two comrades trapped in the room were brought out later.

London Fights the Robots

Ernest Hemingway must have experienced a mixture of emotions in London in July 1944. He had been sent over as a war correspondent to cover the D-Day landings for *Collier's* magazine and found that the movie of his novel, *For Whom the Bell Tolls*, starring Gary Cooper, had just opened in the capital. Hemingway, though, was a man with a nose for a story – especially one where bravery and courage were involved – and found both when he met some of the pilots involved in the war against the flying bombs. Not only did he get a chance to visit the RAF bases where these operations were being carried out, he also flew on a bombing raid against the V-1 sites in France. In his report, written in mid-July but not published in *Collier's* until 19 August, he talks of meeting a squadron leader and a wing commander. Though neither are named, they were, in fact, Squadron Leader Joseph Berry and Wing Commander Roland Beaumont. This essay undoubtedly did much to make Americans fully aware of the extraordinary battle that was being waged across the Atlantic against a robot enemy.

The Tempest is a great, gaunt aeroplane. It is the fastest pursuit job in the world and is as tough as a mule. It has been reported with a speed of 400 and should dive way ahead of its own noise. Where we were living, its job was to intercept the pilotless planes and shoot them down over the sea or in open country as they came in on their sputtering roar towards London. The squadron flew from four o'clock in the morning until midnight. There were always pilots sitting ready in the cockpits to take off when the Very pistol signalled, and there were always a number of planes on permanent patrol in the air. The fastest time I clocked a plane as airborne, from the sound of the pop of the flare pistol that would arc a twin flare over toward the dispersal area from the door of the Intelligence hut, was fifty-seven seconds.

As the flare popped, you would hear the dry bark of the starting cartridge and the rising stream of the motor, and these hungry, big, long-legged birds, would lurch, bounce, and scream off with the noise of two hundred circular saws hitting a mahogany log dead on the nose. They took off downwind, crosswind, any way the weather lay, and grabbed a piece of the sky and lurched up into it with the long high legs folding up under them.

You love a lot of things if you live around them, but there isn't any woman and there isn't any horse, nor any before nor any after, that is as lovely as a great aeroplane, and men who love them are faithful to them even though they leave them for others. A man has only one virginity to lose in fighters, and if it is a lovely plane he loses it to, there his heart will ever be. And a P-51 can do something to a man's heart.

Mustang is a tough, good name for a bad, tough, husky, angry plane that could have been friends with Harry Greb if Greb had had an engine instead of a heart. Tempest is a sissy name out of Shakespeare, who is a great man anywhere, but they have put it on to an aeroplane that is sort of like a cross between Man o' War and Tallulah Bankhead in the best year either of them ever had. They were good years, too, and many a man has been taken by the bookies because he looked

115

at a colt that had the swelling Big Red's neck had and not any of the rest of it. And there have been many husky voices since, but none that carried good across the Western ocean.

So now we have this squadron of Tempests. They were running out of terms for meteorological disturbances when they named that one. And all day long they shoot down this nameless weapon, day in and day out. The squadron leader is a fine man, tall, small-spoken the way a leopard is, with the light brown circles under his eyes and the odd purple complexion of a man whose face has been burned away, and he told the story of his exploit to me very quietly and truthfully, standing by the wooden table in the pilots' mess.

He knew it was true and I knew it was true and he was very precise in remembering exactly how it had been, because it was one of the first pilotless aircraft he had shot down, and he was very exact in details. He did not like to say anything personal but it was evidently all right to speak well of the plane. Then he told me about the other sort of shooting down. If you do not explode them in the air, you crash them.

'It is a sort of giant bubble of blast that rises from them,' he said. 'Bubble' had been quite a venturesome word to use, and he took confidence from it and tried a further word. 'It is rather like a huge *blossoming* of air rising.'

We were both embarrassed by this articulateness, and as my mind watched the giant bubble blossoming, all tension was taken away by an American flying in the same squadron, who said, 'I dropped one on a green-house, and the glass rose straight up a million feet. What am I going to say to the guy who owns that greenhouse when we go into the pub tonight?'

'You can't just say exactly where you'll shoot them down,' the squadron leader said, standing there, speaking shyly, patiently and with strange eagerness,

116

from behind the purple mask he would always wear now for a face. 'They go very fast you know.'

The wing commander came in, angry, happy. He was short, with a lot of style and a tough, bad tongue. He was twenty-six, I found out later. I had seen him get out of an aeroplane before I knew he was the wing commander. It did not show then, nor did it show now when he talked. The only way you knew he was the wing commander was the way the other pilots said 'Sir'. They said 'Sir' to the two squadron leaders, one of whom was a tough Belgian like a six-day bicycle racer, and the other was the shy, fine man who lived behind the destroyed face. But they gave a slightly different 'Sir' to the wing commander, and the wing commander returned no change from it at all. Nor did he notice it when he pocketed it.

Censorship, in war, is a very necessary thing. It is especially necessary about aircraft because, until a new aircraft has fallen into enemy hands, no information as to the exact speeds, dimensions, characteristics or armament should be written, since all of that furnishes information the enemy wants and needs.

It is appearance, characteristics and performance that make a man love an aeroplane, and they, told truly, are what put the emotion into an article about one. They are all out of this article now. I hope the enemy never shoots down a Tempest, that the Tempest will never be released from the secret list, and that all I know and care about them can never be published until after the war.

All information about tactics employed in the shooting down of pilotless aircraft is out, too, along with all the conversation that would let you know how the types feel that do the shooting down. Because you cannot have the conversation without conveying the tactics. So there isn't much in this article now, except a guy loving an aeroplane.

It is written in tough language because this was, in the main, a tough-speaking outfit. The only exception was the squadron leader, fragments of whose conversation are given. Some outfits in the RAF are very rough spoken, and some speak as gently and correctly as in the film, *Target for Tonight*. I like ('like' is a very mild term to employ for the emotion felt) both kinds, and sometime, if it is ever possible to write anything interesting that the censor can conscientiously pass, I would like to try to show both kinds. In the meantime you get this.

Writing under censorship is necessary and proper in time of war, and we all censor out ourselves everything we think might be of any possible interest to the enemy. But in writing about the air on the basis of trying to include colour, detail and emotions, there is a certain analogy to sports writing.

It is sort of as though in the old days you had found Harry Greb having a breakfast of double orders of ham and eggs and hashed brown potatoes in bed at nine o'clock in the morning on the day he was to fight Mickey Walker. Greb, placed on the scales, weighed exactly 12 pounds over the 162 he was to make at two o'clock that afternoon. Now suppose you had seen the weight rubbed and pounded off of him and got rid of by several other means, and him carried on the scales too weak to walk and almost too weak to curse you.

Then suppose you had seen the meal he ate and seen him enter the ring weighing exactly the same weight he had left bed with that morning. Then suppose you had seen the great, crowding, smashing, take it, come in again, thumping, butting, mean, nasty, bloody, lovely fight he made, and you had to sum up the whole business in these terms: One of our fighters named Greb whose characteristics have not been revealed was reported to have encountered an M. Walker last night. Further details will be released in due course.

If this ever seems a screwy story, remember that

through the sky at all times are passing pilotless aircraft which look, in flight, rather like an ugly metal dart with a white-hot bunghole, travel at speed up to 400 miles an hour, carry, as of this writing, 2,200 pounds of explosive in their noses, make a noise like a glorified motor-cycle and, at this moment, are passing overhead the place where this is written.

One of my most esteemed colleagues told me in New York that he was not returning to the European theatre because anything he might write would merely be a repetition of what he had already written. At this point I am authorised to state to my esteemed colleague that the danger of repetition in a story is one of the more negligible hazards that his old co-workers are at present confronted with.

Now if you are following this piece closely – which I am not, due to a certain amount of windowpane trouble – we should be somewhere in southern England where a group of Tempest pilots have in seven days shot down their share of pilotless aircraft. Lots of people call this weapon the doodlebug, the robot bomb, the buzz bomb and other names hatched in the brains of the keener Fleet Street types, but so far nobody I have ever known who has fought him has referred to Joe Louis as Toots. So we will continue to refer to this weapon as the pilotless aircraft in this release from your pilotless-aircraft editor, and you can call it any of those quaint or coy names you wish, but only when you are alone.

The day before your pilotless-aircraft editor started studying the interception angle, he or I (I guess it is I, although sometimes it doesn't seem the right man in the right place and I have thought some of leaving the whole thing and going back to writing books in stiff covers), went out in one of forty-eight Mitchell bombers – that is, eight boxes of six bombers each – to bomb one of the sites from which the pilotless aircraft are launched.

These sites can be readily identified by the merest tyro by the quantity of old Mitchell bombers which are strewed around them and by the fact that, when you get close to them, large, black circular rings of smoke appear alongside of the vehicle you are riding in. These circular black rings of smoke are called flak, and this flak is the author of that old piece of understatement about two of our aircraft failed to return.

Well, we (that is Wing Commander Lynn, who is nice company in an aeroplane and who has exactly the same voice on the intercom when Kees, the bombardier, has her held in on the run and is saying, 'Bombing – Bombing – Bombing – Bombing –' as though you were not on the last mile) bombed this site with proverbial pin-point accuracy. I had a nice look at the site which appeared to be a gigantic concrete construction lying on its side or its belly (depending on whether you saw it just before the run or just after it) in a wood completely surrounded by bomb craters. There were two small clouds that didn't look lonely the way the clouds were in 'I wandered lonely as a cloud'.

There were many rings of the black smoke in a line coming right straight alongside of us inside the box between us and where the other Mitchell on our right was going along in the air, looking just like a picture of a Mitchell in an advertisement by the manufacturers. Then, with the smoke rings forming along her side, the belly of this kite – looking just like in moving pictures – opened, pushing out against the air, and the bombs all dropped out sideways as if she were having eight long metal kittens in a hurry.

We all were doing this, although you could not see what anybody did except this one. Then we all went home just as fast as we could go home, and that is bombing. Unlike a lot of other things, the best part is afterward. I suppose it is something like going to college. It isn't so much how much you learn. It is the wonderful people you meet.

Your pilotless-aircraft editor never went to college (here we call it a university), so now he is going to the RAF instead, and the main subject he is studying is trying to understand English on the radio telephone. Face to face with an Englishman, I can understand almost everything he says. I can speak, read and write Canadian clearly and have a smattering of Scottish and a few words of New Zealand. I can understand enough Australian to draw cards and order drinks and to shove my way into a bar if it is crowded. South African I dominate as a spoken tongue almost as well as I do Basque. But English over the RT is just a glorious mystery.

Close up, over the intercom in a bomber, I get most of it. When you press the button on the stick, that isolates conversation to what is said in the cockpit, so you have those long, intimate chats that go, 'Wonder who that b— is that's talking,' and you answer, 'Don't know. Must be the same Jerry that on the night of D-Day kept saying "Turn back. Turn back. The operation has been cancelled!"'

'Wonder how he gets on our wave length?'

You shrug your shoulders and take your thumb off the button. That close conversation I get all right, but when the real Englishmen speaking English start talking to one another between one kite and another kite and back and forth from control, I just study it hard like homework, as if you had brought home somebody's calculus book and were still on plane geometry.

Actually, I cannot understand English very well yet on the ordinary telephone, so, having been indoctrinated in the Good Neighbour policy, I always say, 'Yes', and just make them repeat the time the car will be around in the morning to take us to whatever field we will be starting from.

This accounts for many of the curious sorties your

pilotless-aircraft correspondent goes on. He is not a man who has a perpetual urge to seek peril in the sky or to defy the laws of gravity; he is simply a man who, not understanding very well the nature of the propositions offered over the telephone due to faulty earwork, constantly finds himself involved in the destruction of these monsters in their hellish lairs or in attempts at interception in that fine, 400-mile-an-hour aeroplane, the Mosquito.

At present, your pilotless-aircraft editor has stopped all telephone calls of any description in order to attempt to bring the story up to date before someone proposes something so startling and so generous to your editor in the nature of an operation that he would fail in his duties to this great book to have recorded what has happened up to this time. However, before all calls were stopped, two or three rather lovely propositions were received, and I understand that there is a feeling freely expressed in some quarters that, 'Ernie is yellow. With a chance to go on absolutely wizard ops, he is up in his room at that pub, doing what do you think?'

'What?' in a horrified tone.

'Writing.'

'My God! The old boy's had it!'

A tribute in return to some American servicemen who became involved in a flying-bomb incident in London appeared in *The Times* at the same time as Ernest Hemingway was writing his piece. It took the form of a letter to the Editor by a Mrs B Ruthven-Murray of Newman Street, and read as follows:

I happened recently to be at the scene of an incident. I was much struck by two features of it. One was the way sightseers rushed from all directions to the scene and formed themselves into solid, wedged masses, so that it was practically impossible for Civil Defence personnel and vehicles to approach without having to fight their way through, thus causing delays with tragic consequences.

'The other was the way American troops in the neighbourhood rallied round to help. Before many minutes a line of jeeps was formed to take the injured to hospital and apparently without formal authority a number of soldiers threw a cordon at one point to stem the flow of the surging crowd and divert and regulate the traffic. I think there is a lesson to be learned from each of these events.'

Life in Underground City

The writer to *The Times* was not the only person a little unhappy about the behaviour of some people in London during the flying-bomb attacks. George Orwell, who had not yet written *1984* but was already well known for *Down and Out in Paris and London* as well as his strong views on Socialism, observed several features of life that disturbed him and wrote a controversial essay for the July issue of the *Partisan Review*. In it he compared existence in the city to that of the days of the Blitz and worried, in particular, about the future for the younger generation.

This has been a foul summer, everything happening at the wrong time and hardly any fruit. The countryside has quite changed its face, the once-green meadows having changed into cornfields, and in the remotest places one cannot get away from the roar of airplanes, which has become the normal background noise. I have been tied so tightly to this beastly town that for the first time in my life I have not heard a cuckoo this year...

After the wail of the siren comes the zoom-zoom-zoom of the flying bomb, and as it draws nearer you get up from your table and squeeze yourself into some corner that flying glass is not likely to reach. Then, BOOM!, the windows rattle in their sockets and you go back to work.

There is very little political news. All the currents seem to be moving in the same directions – public opinion leftward, the Right nevertheless consolidating its power owing to the weakness of the Labour leaders, and the minor left-wing parties quarrelling among themselves.

There is violent competition by all parties to cash in on the popularity of the USSR. The pinks depreciate any criticism of the USSR on the ground that it 'plays into the hands of the Tories', but on the other hand the Tories seem to be the most pro-Russian of the lot. From the point of view of the MOI and the BBC the only two people who are completely sacrosanct are Stalin and Franco.

I imagine that the Russians themselves regard the Tories as their real friends in the country. It may possibly be of some significance that the Soviet press recently made a sharp attack on a group of very Russophile left-wing MPs who had made the suggestion that the flying bombs were manufactured in Spain! These MPs included D.N. Pritt, the alleged 'underground' Communist who has been perhaps the most effective pro-Soviet publicist in this country.

There are a few social developments, which again take the same directions as I reported before. Evening dress (i.e. for men) is gradually reappearing. The distinction between first and third class on the railways is being enforced again. Two years ago it had practically lapsed. Commercial advertisements which I told you a year or so back were rapidly disappearing, are definitely on the up-grade again and make use of the snobbery motif more boldly.

The Home Guard still exists in as great numbers as before, but is employed largely on the AA guns and seems now to have no political colour of one kind or another. It now consists to a great extent of youth who are conscripted in at 16 or 17. For boys younger than

this there are various cadet corps and the Air Training
Corps, and even for young girls a uniformed formation
named vaguely the Girls' Training Corps. All this is
something quite new in English life, pre-military
training having been practically confined to the middle
and upper classes before the war.

Everything grows shabbier and more rickety. Sixteen
people in a railway carriage designed for ten is quite
common. There are disgusting scenes in the Tube
stations at night, sordid piles of bedding cluttering up
the passageways and hordes of dirty-faced children
playing around the platforms at all hours.

Two nights ago, about midnight, I came on a little
girl of five 'minding' her younger sister, aged about two.
The tiny child had got hold of a scrubbing brush with
which she was scrubbing the filthy stones of the
platform, and then sucking the bristles.

I took it away from her and told the elder girl not to
let her have it. But I had to catch my train, and no
doubt the poor little brat would again be eating filth in
another couple of minutes. This kind of thing is
happening everywhere. However, the disorganisation
and consequent neglect of children hasn't been serious
compared with 1940.

Scarcely had the ink dried on this article, when a reporter
from the *South London Press* infiltrated himself into the
Tube system to see for himself what conditions were like
and write the following exclusive story on Friday, 14 July.
'No reporter has been officially allowed to visit the deep
shelters since they were opened this week,' an editorial
introduced the article. 'The Ministry of Home Security will
not give its permission. Disregarding this Whitehall ukase,
which is resented by the Borough Councils concerned, a
South London Press reporter borrowed a shelterer's ticket
and below he gives his story.'

126

I slept on Wednesday night in the first deep shelter to be opened in Stockwell, an underground city for 8,000 people, 150 feet down. About 4,000 people are sleeping here each night and thousands more are queuing, hours at a time, for tickets which do not arrive.

I agree with the shelterers to whom I talked that it is a fine piece of work. Built on a Tube planned for post-war development, it stretches for miles beneath South London, a system of tunnels criss-crossing main tunnels, well-lit, air-conditioned, warm (most people are satisfied with the temperature now), white-painted.

No one seems to know how many the whole shelter will hold, but the section now open, with room for about 8,000, is by no means the largest. 65,000 is one warden's estimate.

I showed my ticket to the warden at the entrance and went down 200 steps. Notices directed shelterers to their sections and I soon found my bunk, part of a 'family' section of two double and one single bunks. I left my coat and blankets and followed signposts to the canteen. A shillingsworth of tickets from the paybox gave me supper and breakfast. Prices are low – tea 2d., cake 2d., sandwiches 2d., cocoa 2d.

From 10 p.m. to 11 p.m. I walked up and down the tunnels – it takes seven minutes to cover two sections – smoked a cigarette and arranged a bed for myself.

At 10.40 p.m. a warden called 'Lights out in five minutes.' At 10.50 four out of every five lights went out and five minutes later the remaining lights were dimmed. By 11.15 everyone had settled down.

The only sounds were the padding of patrols of wardens (all voluntary) and the rumbling of the Tube trains faint overhead.

At three next morning the 'early caller' – a warden who sees that workers are called on time – came round and by 5.30 half the shelterers were awake again.

At 6.30 there were queues at the canteen for

breakfast. I asked a warden by what time I had to leave. 'Everyone out by eight,' he said, 'to give the cleaners a chance.'

By eight the team of cleaners were preparing for the next night. They hadn't much to do – Deep City is cleaner than the London above and the only litter I saw was cigarette ends. They were there because there are no ashtrays (the only omission) in the underground city.

Death on a Monday Morning

In the summer of 1944 the alternative to crowding into an underground refuge – or your own Anderson or Morrison shelter – to escape from the flying bombs was to get out of the London area altogether. Some families just packed their bags and used their own resources to leave, but from Saturday, 5 July the Government also instituted an official evacuation scheme of its own.

Strictly speaking, the evacuation scheme was 're-opened' for it had never really stopped since the days of the Blitz in 1940, and statistics reveal that just prior to the beginning of the doodlebug war there were still something like 300,000 official refugees, mothers and children, living in the north of the country far away from the dangers of the big cities.

But once the V-1s began to fall and Greater London became a hell of explosions, falling buildings and the even more terrifying showers of splintered glass, many families – especially those where the father was away fighting – understandably became afraid for their lives, and the number of evacuees trebled so that by early September over one million had left the area. The highest priority in the Government's scheme – which was totally voluntary – was given to mothers with babies and pregnant women; then came children under five (especially those orphaned or in residential nurseries); school children between the ages of five and sixteen; and finally family units and old people.

Blackpool was the destination of the first 2,400 evacuees to leave London on 5 July, and within two days another 16,500 mothers, babies and young children had been despatched by trains and buses to the West Country, Shropshire, the Midlands, Lancashire and even as far afield as Scotland: all places where the V-1 had not only never been seen but was also an unknown quantity.

The experiences of these Londoners in their new surroundings were often a repeat of what had happened in the first great evacuation brought about by the Blitz. Quite a few of the children were older now, though, and more amenable about being transported into what had originally seemed like an alien culture where milk came from cows and not a bottle, and potatoes were dug up from the ground and not picked from a greengrocer's box. Four years of war had not only broadened their knowledge of life but also hardened them to the pain of losing parents killed on the battlefields or, more tragically still, in the familiar streets of their homes.

Their stories have, in fact, been told in detail in a number of books, but as this is a volume primarily about the effect of the flying bombs on London, what about those who chose to remain? The children whose parents decided to brave it out in their own homes in defiance of the worst Hitler could throw at them? My own story is, I believe, typical of many.

This aspect of the war years has a special poignancy for me because I was one of those children who was born when London first came under the German bombardment in 1940, and I remember four years later the sight of a V-1 passing over my home just moments before it exploded. It is, in fact, my only clear recollection of the war, and I know that there are a great many other men and women of the same age who share similar experiences.

Admittedly our home was at Enfield on the northern fringes of London, which was then a more countrified area than it is today. But the fact remains that there were many flying bombs which overshot their target of Central London and plunged onto places such as Enfield. And those youngsters who survived to tell the story have no cause to regret the decision of their parents not to move.

I had not long had my fourth birthday when the V-1 came into my life on the morning of Monday, 26 June 1944. My father, who was in the RAF, had been posted abroad and was then in Egypt serving on ground control at Cairo. My mother – as she has from time to time reminded me – had her hands full raising a lively small boy who displayed no fear at the sight of enemy aircraft passing overhead and slept through every night-time raid or explosion.

My mother, an intensely practical woman, says she also remembers the day of the V-1 because it marked the start of a new Ration Period and it had just been announced that there was to be a reduction of one third in the points value of sardines and tinned rabbit. Such things obviously meant nothing to me, although I do like sardines but have never had much of a taste for rabbit, tinned or otherwise.

The day started unremarkably enough. I was playing contentedly with some toys in the garden when a noise that sounded like a motor-car engine caught my attention. The strange thing was that the car seemed to be up in the air.

I looked over the rows of apple trees at the end of our garden and saw what seemed like an aeroplane coming towards me. But as it grew nearer, I could see that it had only tiny wings and there appeared to be flames coming out of its tail.

I watched mesmerised as the thing got nearer, the noise drumming on my ears. Suddenly, I felt a pair of arms grab hold of me. It was my mother, and without a word she picked me up and began running up the garden towards the house.

Totally unaware of the danger I was in, I began to struggle in her arms and protest. I wanted to see the funny aeroplane, I cried. Wisely, she did not waste breath arguing, but rushed me into the house and pushed us both into a little cupboard under the stairs.

Although I cannot be quite sure of the fact after all these years, I believe my last sight of the missile as we went

131

through the back door was the moment it fell silent and began its plunge to earth. What I *do* remember is the muffled sound of an explosion some moments later from the other side of the cupboard door where we were both crouched.

When all was still once more, we emerged into the daylight again. My mother made no protest when I ran to the back door and looked out. There was nothing to see now, save a pillar of smoke curling up above the apple trees.

'What was that, Mummy?' I asked.

'A Buzz-Bomb,' she told me, returning again to her kitchen chores, 'they are very dangerous. We have to come indoors when they go overhead.'

'Where do they come from?' I said.

'The Germans,' she said tightening her lips. 'The people who have taken Daddy away from us.'

She might just as well have told me the rocket had come from the Moon for all the mention of 'the Germans' meant. But I did appreciate the danger, because I knew my daddy would not have been away from us for so long unless *something* was wrong. I just hoped that he would do something about those Germans and their nasty machines and come home...

I certainly might not have been here to tell this story had the flying bomb landed nearer our home, and it was not until some years later that I learned what had happened to it. For unlike a number of the other V-1s which had dropped onto open spaces in Enfield, that particular one had made a direct hit on the home of the town clerk, a Mr George E Malley, completely wrecking the building. Mrs Malley had been killed instantly by the explosion and her husband had died later in hospital.

The death of those two innocent victims by the bomb that I had seen with my own eyes added a new dimension to my memories...

While I was researching this book, I was interested to discover in the newspapers for that same June day a number of accounts about other children who had had encounters with flying bombs, most of them far more dangerous than my own. Naturally I collected them all and I would like to include a few samples here, beginning with one from *The Times*, headed 'Children's Calmness At School', which like all such stories from the period is frustratingly non-commital as to the location:

'Nearly 100 children at a private school escaped serious injury yesterday when a flying bomb fell in a garden close by,' *The Times* reported. 'The children were at their lessons at the time. Every window in the school was smashed, doors were torn off, and furniture was thrown about, but the children remained calm. A number of pupils and two teachers were injured by flying glass, but a boy with an eye injury was the only one detained in hospital.'

A not dissimilar report in the *Daily Telegraph* stated: 'Children at a south of England school had a narrow escape yesterday when a flying bomb fell on the playing fields adjoining the building. The pupils were on their way to a shelter and showed no panic. Three children and one teacher were taken to hospital with cuts from flying glass.'

The *Daily Express* had an equally interesting tale for its readers: 'A raid drill in the event of a V-1 attack actually saved some children at a school in southern England yesterday when one of the bombs really fell. They were in their classrooms when the missile came down and they filed out to their shelters just as if it were a routine drill. No one was injured, although damage was done to the buildings by the blast.'

A fourth item I clipped from the *News Chronicle* contained perhaps the most dramatic story of all: 'A number of boys were asleep in their dormitories when a flying bomb dropped near their school in the south of England yesterday. The blast broke almost every window, but not a single child was injured. Nor were the patients in a hospital for sick children when it, also, was damaged by a blast. The staff, too, escaped injury.'

My research also brought to light another specific account from Enfield about a girl who was taking her School

Certificate on that Monday, 26 June. The story has been told by the wartime historian Norman Longmate who quotes the young lady herself:

'There were air raids nearly all day and we had to keep hopping under our desks when the doodlebugs came along,' she recalled. 'I couldn't concentrate. The French unseen wasn't bad but the prose was not very good and I wrote an idiotic essay. I remember sitting in the cloakroom at lunch-time eating sandwiches because there was an alert on.

'The conditions next day were even worse and we lost so much time getting under the desks when an alert was on we were allowed ten minutes extra. I was told later that a special report was sent to the examining board about the flying bombs so that extra marks could be added for the disturbance factor.'

Just like me, that girl – half a century and a life-time of experiences later – still remembers her encounter with the flying bombs with a clarity that speaks volumes about their impact on our young lives.

Among my contemporaries who have flying-bomb stories to tell, one of the most unusual is that of Cecil Smith, with whom I worked in publishing for a number of years, and who was a child living in Carshalton, Surrey at the same time as I was living in Enfield. Cecil's semi-detached home in a typical middle-class area was almost exactly the same distance to the south of Central London as mine was to the north, which gives an added interest to his account as well as further underlining how often wildly off target the German V-1 launchers still were in August 1944. 'It happened at a time when there were a lot of flying bombs coming over,' Cecil told me, 'and hardly a night went by without the sirens going off. My parents and some of our neighbours spent most evenings in our house while about nine other children and I slept in the Anderson shelter in our garden.

'One night I was in the shelter when I heard the sound of

a doodlebug going overhead and I just couldn't resist the temptation to stick my head out of the door to have a look. You see, there were no grown-ups to stop me and the flying bombs were a bit of a game to all of us youngsters, anyhow. Well, I looked out and saw this huge black shape with flames pouring out of the end right overhead. The engine stopped and even as I jumped back into the shelter and slammed shut the door, I could hear it hitting a house a couple of doors away from ours.

'There was an enormous explosion and then all hell let loose. We felt a terrific tremor and when we opened the shelter door we could see that the whole of the back of our house had been blown away and the wall had fallen onto where we were hiding. But for the strength of that shelter we would all have been crushed flat.

'I remember that my brother Leslie ran straight out of the shelter and stepped onto a red-hot piece of metal that badly burnt his foot. And then I saw my mother who was carrying my baby sister Margaret emerging from the ruins of the kitchen. Behind her there was one of our neighbours all covered in glass. I later found out that this woman had panicked and tried to get out of the house as the bomb fell. She had pushed past my mother just as the back door had been blown in, showering her with hundreds of glass splinters. If she had stayed where she was the blast would have hit my mother and her baby.

'That night all we children were sent away to another shelter while the rescue workers did what they could. At least half a dozen of the houses had been destroyed and a couple of people killed. But perhaps the biggest surprises of all came when I went back to the house the next day.

'The explosion had caused a wardrobe belonging to my father to be literally blown out of his bedroom down the garden and it had ended up in the branches of an apple tree! And when we began to root around in the house to salvage some of our possessions, my mother was horrified to find that the place had been looted during the night. Someone had actually ransacked our home and stolen some money from a desk drawer. I still find it difficult to believe anyone could have done that to people who had just lost everything!

'Obviously, we couldn't live in the house and it had to be pulled down and completely rebuilt. In the meantime we were all evacuated to Sheffield, where most people had hardly even heard of a flying bomb let alone come anywhere near as close to death as we had done that night.'

It's an Ill Wind

As August drew to a close, the joint efforts of the RAF and AA were scoring increasing successes against the flying bombs and there was a growing feeling that the worst of the attacks might soon be over – especially as the Allied Forces were now daily pushing deeper into France and closer to the German border. On 28 August, for instance, the English defensive forces brought down 90 of the 97 V-1s reported approaching England, and of the remainder only four reached Greater London. The newspapers were happy to record these successes, and the general sense of optimism was typified by articles such as 'It's An Ill Wind' written by the editor of *Punch*, E V Knox, known to his readers as 'Evoe', for the issue of 28 August. The feelings of optimism even rose so high early in September as to inspire a rumour in London that the Germans were on the point of suing for peace: a story which made the front page of the *Daily Herald* of 5 September and which is reprinted here immediately after 'Evoe's' amusing contribution.

The story that a Kent farmer had all the apples conveniently knocked off a tree he was about to pick owing to the blast caused by a flying bomb, was so swiftly followed by the headline

BABY'S LIFE SAVED BY A DOODLEBUG

that I began to think deeply and remember how often

what appears to be a nuisance, or far worse, may prove to be a blessing in disguise.

The baby (in case you did not read about it) had turned itself over and was lying face downwards in the pillow of its perambulator. Alarmed by the noise overhead its mother raced to wheel it to some safer place, and was thus able to rescue it from almost certain suffocation. Once more the doodlebug was doing the good deed for the day.

I began thereupon to collect instances of noble and virtuous actions committed (in spite of their own evil hearts) by unpiloted planes and I found that I had not far to go.

In a very well-known part of Southern England I met a very notorious sailor who told me that he had just mixed two cocktails and put them down on the window-sill of his dining-room when the usual commotion occurred. He took refuge with his wife in the passage, and when all was over and the block of flats had shaken as he said 'like a jelly', or no, he corrected himself, 'like an aspen leaf', they went back to drink their drinks, and found that though the glasses were unbroken and unmoved, the power of suction, following the blast, had taken every drop of liquid out of them and spilled it on the floor.

'But that,' I said, 'was bad, unless you were about to reform. This bomb of yours was practically behaving like a Pussyfoot.'

'You might think so,' he said, 'but later we gave a glass of this gin mixed with lime juice to a friend, and he had to be taken to hospital. It was wood-alcohol of the worst. I shall always count that bomb as the agent of a benign though mysterious Providence.'

Another friend of mine had a collection of the ugliest pictures in the world totally destroyed by a similar miracle, while the photographs of his aunt, a most excellent woman, of whom he had high expectations, remained wholly intact.

Or shall I rather tell, now that I have begun to bomb-bore you, of the man whose window was blown in and all his correspondence torn to shreds and tatters by the flail of the flying enemy?

'That surely was a misfortune,' I argued in my simplicity.

'No, not entirely,' he said. 'One of the notes I had written was a letter to *The Times* explaining how W. G. Grace had struck a fast ball at Lord's which totally disappeared from view. The umpire was obliged to give six runs for the stroke, and it was not until a week later the ball was found in the mazes of the Master's beard, where he had not noticed it. Apparently he only combed his beard out every Wednesday.'

'I don't see—' I said.

'Well, I don't mind telling you that this story was a downright lie. *The Times* was saved from publishing it, and I was saved from sin.'

Or of that other man shall I tell who had just posted a false return of his income tax when the pillar-box to which he had entrusted it was entirely swept away? Or of the man who was blown with his bed and all into the street and woke up in the morning to find that every brick of his home had disappeared? 'I never liked that house anyway,' he said with a quiet smile of satisfaction.

His watch, which was under his pillow, had always gained. It was still ticking, but thereafter kept perfect time; I think that must be true, because he has shown me the watch.

And look you how many a hasty speech has been begun, how many an idle word that might have pained the hearer has been left unuttered owing to the arrival of a flying bomb. It is impossible to continue a conversation with a sarcastic smile, or a wounding intonation, when one is lying on the floor with one's head in the waste-paper basket.

From still another part of Southern England comes the story of a man who was flying from an enraged bull when a doodlebug tossed him gently into the upper branches of an elm-tree, and so terrified the animal that it has never been the same bull, if it ever was, as formerly. Or it may have been a cow. I think it was a cow and from that day onward it has yielded milk of a higher grade than it ever conceded before.

There are people also I find who have begun to like the sirens. They are not happy when sirens are not sounding. Far from enjoying the 'merciful lull', as the daily papers are too apt to call it, they become bored and restless and disagreeable, and are only their bright selves again when the air is full of wailing and the skies begin to rattle above. Or they think V-2 is coming and that V-2 may make a sillier noise than V-1.

Myself I am not like this. I am capable of great terror and I shall proceed to relate the story of the worst shock I have received since the curious visitation began. I had been sent to collect some greengrocery in a basket because 'the boy had not been'. Boys in my experience never have. Suddenly there rose an uproar so tremendous that I leapt in the air, dropping my basket on the pavement. I was not really familiar with that small and rather dingy street, and I thought at first that my head had been blown off and my inside removed. The deafening terror came at me very low down and apparently some fifteen yards away. It was the siren, blowing 'All Clear'. Even here there was solace for my sudden fright, for the vegetables, including four tomatoes, had rolled far in the gutter. In the depth of my heart I hate tomatoes and can seldom have too few.

Let us never forget, then, that we have all much to be thankful for. Some of the very worst books that might ever have appeared in print have been destroyed by these robots while still in manuscript, and many an article even more tiresome than this has been cut short even as this one, owing to the sudden advent of a flying bomb.

But, before I go under, 'A peach tree in the garden of Mr Owen Bridges, of Albert Street, Southern England, has borne six hundred and twelve peaches,' says my morning paper. I know. I know. All of them fell into his lap owing to the action of a doodlebug.

Evoe

RUMOUR SAID, 'IT'S PEACE'

Rumour upon rumour swept through London yesterday. Germany had capitulated; the King was to broadcast; Parliament had been recalled.

Not one of these rumours was true, but they spread from London to the suburbs, and the suburbs passed them on to the provinces.

People left their suburban homes and came to town to join in the 'celebrations'. There were taxis full of singing soldiers and girls everywhere. There were stories that barricades were being put up in Piccadilly to control the overjoyed crowd. Here and there flags even popped out.

In newspaper offices the telephones never stopped ringing. 'Is it true? Is it really true?' callers asked. And it was the same at Broadcasting House. 'The King-to-broadcast' rumour sent officials to the limit – they rang up Buckingham Palace to ask, 'Please do you know anything about a royal broadcast?'

Rumour Tuesday was born at midday like this. Fleet Street newspaper offices received a message from a news agency which declared: 'The Brussels radio announcer today said, "Ladies and gentlemen, foreign stations have announced this morning at about 9.30 the news of the capitulation of Germany. At the present time we have not yet received any confirmation of this news."

Then a little later came this flash: 'Brussels radio has killed the rumour in a message saying: "We are obliged

141

to tell you to our deep regret that the rumour according to which Germany was alleged to have capitulated and which was this morning broadcast by foreign radio stations has not been confirmed. The fight goes on."

But one London evening newspaper had already rushed the first message into its Stop Press column and the news whirled around the West End. I was in a tavern when it was telephoned through. Everyone went joy-crazy.

Three American soldiers set about buying the tavern for us. Everybody bought everybody else a drink. There was a rush for the telephone to spread the news.

For nine minutes it was...PEACE. Then came the denial, and another crop of rumours.

The first was that the BBC had announced at 1 p.m. that the nation should stand by for a special announcement. We listened in...nothing.

Again at 3 p.m. more telephone calls. 'The BBC is going to make a special announcement at 4 p.m.' We listened in...nothing again.

At 5 p.m. a message from an RAF officer; 'Definitely a special announcement at 5.30 p.m.' We listened in...to Bow Bells.

SHAEF then put out its own comment, 'The rumours are untrue. The capitulation of Germany is what we are fighting for, but so far as we know there is no truth in this rumour.'

Then the report that the King was to broadcast last night...and that Parliament had been recalled. Once again the phone calls and the same story, 'No, it isn't true!'

A Lull Before the Storm

On 1 September the last flying bomb was dispatched by German troops from France. Unbeknownst, obviously, to the people of Britain, these soldiers salvaged what they could from falling into the hands of the advancing Allies and fled into Holland where it was planned to continue the launchings. One immediate result of this move was a lull of several days in the number of V-1s reaching England. German records captured after the war revealed that by this date approximately 9,000 flying bombs – including more than 2,000 abortive or bad shots – had been fired at England from France since the opening of the attacks in mid-June. Similar British records indicate that over the same period the defensive forces had brought down 3,563 of the 6,725 bombs approaching the United Kingdom. There was, though, no denying that London had still paid a high price: 2,300 bombs had fallen on the city, killing 6,184 people and seriously injuring another 18,000.

Despite the absence of doodlebugs in the skies, it was not until Thursday, 7 September that the British Government felt confident enough to announce to the people that the war of the flying bomb was over.

Intelligence sources had now confirmed the move of the launching troops to Holland, and every day dozens of the abandoned 'ski sites' were falling into Allied hands. Duncan Sandys, the Chairman of the War Cabinet Committee who had masterminded the battle against the V-1, called a press conference on that Thursday and told journalists, 'Except possibly for a few last shots, the Battle of London is over – we have beaten Hitler's secret weapon, the V-1, which was to have terrorised Britain into making a negotiated peace.'

Reading a prepared statement, Mr Sandys went on to give a resumé of how the RAF fighters and bombers had countered the main threat of the V-1, and the AA and Balloon Barrage had blunted their attacks still further. He also paid tribute to the work of Air Marshal Roderick Hill, General Sir Frederick Pile, and Air Vice-Marshal W C Gell and their men and women in the air and on the ground. At the end of the statement when Mr Sandys invited questions, a shadow seemed to fall over the otherwise convivial assembly. If the threat of the V-1 was now over, he was asked by one reporter, what about the V-2?

'I am a little chary of talking about the V-2,' the minister said after a pause. 'We do know quite a lot about it. In a very few days' time I feel that the Press will be walking all over these places in France and we will know a great deal more then than we do now.'

Duncan Sandys was certainly right in predicting that correspondents would soon be sending dispatches about the German launching sites in France – as the two reports by Lawrence Fairhall of the *Daily Sketch* and Frank Gillard for BBC radio graphically reveal. But as to knowing 'a great deal more' about the rocket weapon...what neither Mr Sandys nor anyone else in Britain knew at that moment was that the beginning of the second stage of Hitler's *Vergeltungswaffe* campaign was now only a matter of hours away.

THE STORY FROM THE LAUNCHING SITES
By Lawrence Fairhall

'Suddenly there is a terrific explosion like a hundred bombs going off. Windows in the houses and cottages for miles around rattle; others near by are blown into a thousand fragments by the concussion.

'The sky and surrounding countryside are lit up with a blinding flash of fiery red light, and an object like a meteor races across the heavens with the roar of an express train.'

That is how several French people describe the take-off of a flying bomb.

'It is a terrifying spectacle,' said one of them. 'There is an explosion which deafens you.

'Then the robot shoots across the sky like a ball of fire. Cattle bellow with fear and everyone falls flat to the ground in case it does not work properly.'

A great number of the flying bombs never took off at all. They exploded on the sites, blowing up everything within range of the blast.

Lying in the fields in the vicinity of two sites I visited at Montigny and St Jean du Cardonnay, outside Rouen, were the remains of dozens of flying bombs which had travelled only a mile or so before hitting the ground.

According to the local inhabitants the German soldiers launching them were terrified. They offered French civilians 1,000 francs a day if they would launch them. On some sites they employed Russian prisoners of war for the job.

The sites I visited were put into operation only a month ago. They were both sited in a thick wood which gave them perfect cover from air reconnaissance.

Where it had been necessary to remove live trees, artificial ones were put in their place when the work of construction had been completed.

The actual launching platform consisted of two rails ten feet apart and about 150 feet in length. At one end was built a pill-box of 3-foot thick concrete.

This contained the switch which fired the launching gear. Operations were observed through a peep-hole.

From what I could gather, the bomb is placed on a giant carrier gear which holds the propellant explosive and runs down the two rails. When it is launched its two wings, which till then are folded back, open out.

This ingenious arrangement enables the weapon to be used in confined spaces, such as a forest, affording the best natural camouflage.

The heat generated during the take-off operation must be intense, as all the trees and shrubs within a few yards of the launching site were blackened and scorched.

At one of the sites a brick wall standing at the end of the launching platform was completely blackened and showed signs of being scorched.

All the buildings on the sites, as well as the intricate machinery employed for launching, are completely mobile, and can be removed within a matter of 12 to 24 hours.

Actually these two sites took less than five weeks to build, including the laying of about 10,000 square yards of concrete. Slave labour from Belgium and Holland was employed.

It is impossible to estimate the exact number of sites which have already fallen into Allied hands, but at a rough guess I should say it was about one hundred. At least a score or more are falling into our hands daily.

SPANNERS IN THE WORKS
By Frank Gillard

While I was being given a conducted tour of the area of northern France recently taken by the Allied Forces, which was not very far from the front, I had the opportunity of hearing how a group of French patriots had been sabotaging some of the flying bombs launched from their soil.

Just a couple of miles from Boulogne we found the Germans making a stand and our jeep was ordered to go back. Half a mile away we pulled in to the side of the road under an embankment to eat our sandwiches.

There was a house by the roadside, and to my surprise the housewife came out and asked if she could do anything for us. Had we food? Had we drink? Well, at least we must allow her to make us a cup of coffee – she said she had been saving coffee since 1939 for this moment.

Think of that – a battle going on half a mile off and this Frenchwoman, not sheltering in her cellar or in some ditch, but insisting on giving us coffee! We went into her house, and there in the living room, in his shirtsleeves, was the local Resistance movement leader with a pair of headphones clamped over his head, listening on a crystal set to the BBC's French Service from London giving the one o'clock news.

He told me that the Germans had planned to build six hundred flying-bomb sites in his area. Many had already been in use. Work had started on them almost exactly a year ago.

The Germans went to a lot of trouble, he said, to make them non-magnetic, so they would be difficult to locate by instruments. But the French who were compelled to work on them filled their pockets each morning with any scraps of iron they could lay their hands on, nails, bits of wire – they even took the hinges off their doors in some cases – and worked all this metal into the concrete when the German bosses had their backs turned.

The man added that as the Germans rushed away when the Allied Forces got closer, going like a lot of tramps, some on stolen bicycles but most of them on foot, pushing their belongings in perambulators and wheelbarrows, he and his friends rejoiced not only in their own liberty, but because the enemy's departure meant that there were six hundred bomb ramps or potential bomb ramps the less to trouble their friends and allies over in England.

147

The Resistance leader told me he believed that it would not be long before all the flying-bomb sites were in Allied hands, and that would mean the end of another chapter of German terror tactics against the people of England.

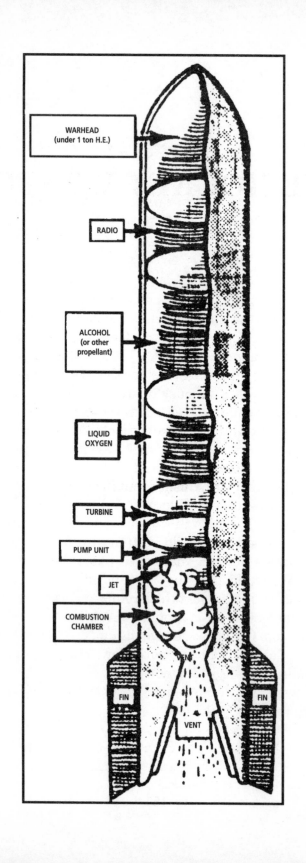

Part II
THE ROCKET WEAPON

All this Spring and Summer our reconnaissance aircraft have brought us photographs of some mysterious half-underground works which the Germans were building along the Channel coast. They were far bigger than the hundred or so launching sites for the flying bomb, which the enemy was also busy with, and which we were attacking. We could not tell exactly what these monstrous sites were, but we did not like the look of them, so we went for them, at first with ordinary bombs. The American Fortresses knocked out one of them at a place called Watten, before it was finished; but in other cases, notably at two places called Wizernes and Mimoyecques, the enemy pushed on with the work in spite of the bombing, and soon began to rebuild Watten also. Finally, we got very detailed air reconnaissance photographs of these places. We found that they were all different. Some of them had walls of 26-foot thick reinforced concrete, going down 100 feet into the ground, and with 26 foot of roof over the top. Others were tunnels dug deep into the hills of the Pas de Calais, with low concrete cupolas protruding. We still did not know exactly what these places were, but we suspected that they had something to do with the enemy's long-range weapon, the V-2.

Squadron Leader John Strachey
Radio broadcast, November 1944

Like a Clap of Thunder

Duncan Sandys had good reason to feel chary at his press
conference about the V-2, for less than thirty-six hours after he
had spoken – and while many people were probably still reading
his statement in their daily newspapers – the first two 'Big
Bens' were launched from Holland and a matter of minutes
later fell on two unsuspecting communities in southern
England. Here, finally, was the deadly rocket that the experts
feared and which both Churchill and Herbert Morrison had
warned the public about. In the Prime Minister's own words,
the weapon was the culmination of almost fifty years of
aerodynamic experiment and was yet another example of
'science now so largely perverted for mass destruction'. Both
Parliamentarians believed the highly destructive V-2 would be
targeted on London in a campaign that might well be
augmented by further use of the flying bomb.

The first two V-2s were fired from Holland on 8
September 1944 and struck within moments of each other –
but at locations some considerable distance apart. Just
which of the pair was the first to land is as much a mystery
as that solo V-1 which may or may not have landed near
Fareham, and this prompted my investigation which is
recounted in the next few pages.

Just as there is an element of mystery surrounding the facts
about precisely when and where the first flying bomb fell on

England, so, too, are there grounds for dispute about the first moment of impact on British soil of its successor, the V-2.

There is no argument among any of the authorities that the first pair of these rocket weapons were launched from The Hague in occupied Holland shortly before seven o'clock in the evening of Friday, 8 September 1944. Nor that both landed within a few minutes of each other about twenty - five miles apart in 'southern England' – as the first communiqué once again put it. It is, though, the matter of those few minutes which is the crux of the argument about which struck first.

Among the various historians who have studied the advent of the V-2, Basil Collier is the most precise about the timing in his book, *The Battle of the V-Weapons*, although this was written in 1964, almost twenty years after the events.

At 6.43 p.m. on that evening, Londoners whom five years of war had made familiar with sudden noises were only mildly startled by a sound which resembled a sharp clap of thunder. At that moment a rocket launched from The Hague about five minutes earlier fell at Chiswick, killing three people and seriously injuring another ten. Sixteen seconds later a second rocket despatched from the same quarter demolished some wooden huts near Epping, but did no other damage and caused no casualties.

At first glance, Mr Collier's facts seem conclusive enough. But are they? For there is an equally strong case that it was the Epping rocket that reached its target first, some four minutes earlier than its deadly companion fell on London.

It is now well established that the British authorities had been expecting a new German secret weapon since January, and just as they had given the V-1 the codename 'Diver', so the term 'Big Ben' was readied for use when these rocket bombs were finally used against the country. Their actual appearance has been neatly summarised by Air Chief

Marshal Sir Philip Joubert who was active in the war effort against them and later wrote a special section on German jet-propelled missiles in his book, *Rocket* (1957).

About the first week of August 1944 the threat of V-2 bombardment had become more definite but against this weapon the only defence was attack. By now our defensive measures had reduced the scale of V-1 attacks to very small proportions. Less than 30 per cent of the bombs launched penetrated the fighter/gun line, and few of these reached London. The limitations of a relatively slow robot-plane flying straight and level had enabled effective countermeasures to be taken against it.

But on 8 September two rockets struck London, one in Chiswick and the other near Epping. By 18 September twenty-five of these projectiles had reached Eastern England and of these fifteen had landed in the London region. Our retaliation against this form of enormously fast weapon was to attack the possible launching areas and the bombing of suspected supply routes and supply depots. There was nothing more that we could do.

During the passage of time since the attack of those first two 'Big Bens', there can be no denying that popular legend has given complete precedence to the Chiswick bomb at the expense of Epping. But there is strong contemporary evidence for the claim of the Essex locality, and what more suitable time to re-examine the facts than at this sixtieth anniversary?

I must confess here that it is a puzzle that has had a particular fascination for me for a long time, because forty-five years ago I started my working life as a young reporter in that very town, Epping. I worked for the weekly *West Essex Gazette* which was then based there, and not only discovered that the newspaper had featured the story of the local V-2 on more than one occasion, but also learned that the event was a recurring topic in local gossip whenever any wartime anniversary came around.

Perhaps to be known as the place where the first German V-2 fell is a rather dubious distinction, and just as I met people in Epping who were indifferent to the argument, so, too, were there people in Chiswick who were not totally convinced they could claim the first rocket. Indeed, this very fact had been made clear in a report in the *Daily Express* as long ago as 27 April 1945, when the bombardment of the 'Big Bens' had ended and reporting restrictions upon its impact were lifted. A clipping from the newspaper of that day explains:

In London the people visited by this new terror weapon debated which was the first that hit them. There was very little time between the first two. One fell in the south of London, the noise of the other came from the north. One was at Chiswick, the other at Epping.

But, curiously, having revealed this debate, the *Express* made no attempt to resolve it as it could so easily have done by using the resources of its reporting staff. They had gone to the trouble of finding out, first-hand, what had happened in Chiswick, but offered not a single word more about the events in Epping.

The paper's report stated:

What happened on 8 September? It was early evening when the whole of London was startled by two terrific explosions. In Staveley Road, Chiswick, the men were taking an evening stroll to the local. Someone was practising scales on the piano in the front room. The women were gossiping at the garden gates. Some others were listening to the radio.

Then the V-2 came. Houses were flattened on either side of the road. A yawning crater 15 feet deep and 30 feet wide opened where a man had been about to cross the road.

'We heard no sound before the explosion rocked the ground,' said the bewildered people in the district. 'There was absolutely no warning like the whistle of a bomb or the chug of a flying-bomb engine. We did not see anything either.'

Eight houses on either side were completely wrecked and many more were severely damaged. The V-2 also claimed its first civilian victim, 65-year-old Mrs Emily Harrison.

Then of the Epping rocket: nothing. So, instead, I turned to the files of my former employers, the *West Essex Gazette*, as well as the memories of local people, to piece together the story of the V-2 that apparently fell almost unnoticed in that quiet rural district in the western corner of Essex.

For generations, Epping has been a market town straddling the B1393 which ran through Epping Forest and on towards what would later become Harlow New Town. Today, it lies in the shadow of the busy junction of the M11 and M25 and has been considerably enlarged by development providing housing for people, many of whom commute daily to London.

In 1944, however, both London and the war itself were somewhat remote from Epping – though, like every other town and village in the country, it had sent men and women off to play their part in the fight against Hitler. If it was known to the public at all, it was probably because of its proximity to the RAF Station at North Weald which had featured so magnificently in the Battle of Britain.

The people of the town had certainly become aware of the flying bombs, for a few which had overshot London had plunged into nearby Epping Forest. (Some of the craters caused by these V-1s still exist today as water-filled ponds, though it is almost impossible to distinguish which are natural and which are explosion-made!) But none of these men and women were prepared for what happened less than a mile from the centre of the town at Epping Upland on the evening of 8 September.

The scene that Friday in the area was actually not that dissimilar to the one in Chiswick. In Epping, the public houses on either side of the main street were already busy with customers having a drink before their evening meals. While in the homes nearby, mothers were cooking dinners, children were having their last games before being called in to eat, and on the radio a selection of cheerful dance band records was being played after yet another satisfying news bulletin of more Allied troop advances in France.

In Epping Upland, about a mile away, a pair of farm workers homeward-bound after a day's ploughing, strolled along the one street and passed a group of children playing around the cluster of small cottages which made up the community.

Not a soul in either of these two places saw or heard anything before the V-2 plunged out of the grey sky at terrifying speed. In Epping, all that anyone was aware of was a sudden, booming explosion somewhere not far away which hurled smoke and debris up into the air. In Epping Upland, the whole ground around Parndon Wood seemed to tremble as if struck by an earthquake. The two men in the street stumbled and fell and several of the children were bowled over as if they had been rag dolls.

The huge explosion from the wood was accompanied by a fall of earth and bits of foliage that rained down on the cottages like some kind of weird storm. Within moments, however, everything was still again – just a pall of white smoke rising steadily above the shattered trees showed that anything untoward had happened.

According to a local story, as one of the two bewildered farm labourers climbed to his feet, helping his companion up as he did so, his gaze happened to stray onto his pocket watch that had fallen from his coat and lay face up on the ground. The hands read exactly 6.40 p.m.

Luckily, apart from a little bruising and some shock, neither of the men nor any of the children were injured by that V-2. There were some wooden storage huts in Parndon

Wood which were completely destroyed and a large crater in the ground bore silent testimony to the force of the explosion. Amidst some uprooted trees the only casualty was found: a rabbit.

Epping Upland had undoubtedly had a miraculous escape from a weapon which, if it had fallen a hundred or so yards closer, would almost certainly have wiped out the entire community.

Details about precisely what kind of bomb had fallen on the wood were to remain a mystery for some weeks. If the people of Epping had their suspicions, they voiced them only to each other – but there was certainly wry amusement when the first official statements about the V-2 bombs landing in England tried to brush them off as exploding gas-mains. For there was no gas-main within miles of Epping Upland in 1944!

Actual public confirmation that it had been a V-2 was provided, as I mentioned earlier, when the embargo on reporting such incidents was lifted in April 1945. But it was not until the November of that year that the first salvo was delivered in the dispute about *where* the first 'Big Ben' fell.

The story started with a reader's letter to the London *Evening News* suggesting that a commemorative plaque should be placed in Staveley Road, Chiswick to mark the spot where the first V-2 had fallen. On reading this, Mrs C Smith of Little Marples Farm in Epping Upland protested to the *Evening News* that if there was to be a memorial of any kind it should be in Epping. But getting no satisfaction there, she decided to take her case to her local paper, the *West Essex Gazette*.

The *Gazette* wasted no time in taking up the cudgels on her behalf, reporting in its issue of 17 November:

Mrs Smith challenged the accuracy of the statement that Chiswick had the first rocket and suggested that the limit of the claim was that it had been the first on

159

London. The London paper maintained that the official view was that Chiswick was the place.

When challenged by Mrs Smith to produce documentary evidence, the *Evening News* replied that having pursued the matter further they were 'assured by the Ministry of Home Security that the first V-2 fell at Chiswick'. It was added that 'apparently there was only a few minutes' difference, but nevertheless it has been set on record that Chiswick was the place'.

Clearly, neither Mrs Smith nor the *Gazette* were satisfied with this answer and the paper decided to set its own reporter on unravelling the mystery. The *Gazette* later carried this report in its columns:

Epping Upland having claimed the doubtful honour as soon as the embargo on information about air raids was lifted at the end of hostilities, our reporter decided to investigate Mrs Smith's challenge. His report says, 'I also contacted the Ministry of Home Security, but I certainly could not get an assurance that it has been officially recorded that Chiswick takes "pride" of place. All I could get, and that unofficially, was that "the first rocket fell at Chiswick in the early evening".

'On turning my attention to official on-the-spot records I find that the Epping ARP Service records a V-2 falling at Parndon Wood, Epping Upland at 6.40 p.m. on 8 September 1944. Chiswick records show its rocket falling at 6.44 p.m.

'It does not seem a wide margin, but four minutes is four minutes, and if the proposal to place something commemorative does materialise, the Ministry of Home Security will have to make up its mind on which record to accept.

Though the *Gazette* returned to the claim again in later issues, stressing the importance of the ARP record and its careful noting of the time of impact, the Chiswick rocket was nonetheless soon enshrined in various histories of the war and it has not been seriously challenged since. In Epping Upland, I was told, there was a general feeling of resignation about 'them London folk claiming things for themselves', and after all the war was now over and it was high time to get on with the real business of life again. Rocket weapons falling from the skies were now just a nasty memory, and that was where they should stay, I was told.

Just how firmly entrenched the London claim now is was demonstrated only recently when the Science Museum ran a poster advertising campaign declaring that the first V-2, which fell on Staveley Road, Chiswick, was 'The First Step to the Moon'.

In Epping, though, there are still a few folk who will insist that the first of the rockets designed by Wernher von Braun, used in anger against England, and then later developed into the Saturn V rocket which took men to the Moon twenty-five years later, actually fell near *them*. As they say, echoing the words of that *Gazette* reporter fifty-seven years ago, 'It does not seem a wide margin, but four minutes *is* four minutes...'

POSTSCRIPT: Epping was hit by another V-2 later in the year when one plunged out of the sky two miles away from the location of the first and hit St Margaret's Hospital on the edge of the town. The missile destroyed the casualty ward but caused only a handful of deaths.

A Tale of Exploding Gas-Mains

Secrecy blanketed the first weeks of the V-2 attacks on
England as the Government attempted to play down their
impact. The first two rockets were soon followed in the next
ten days by further salvoes from Holland, but due to harass-
ment by the Allied bombers and the Germans' lack of
knowledge about their accuracy, only sixteen rockets struck
Greater London, with another eleven finding targets elsewhere in southern England. On 16 September the first flying
bombs for some time were reported in the skies over England,
although these were evidently coming from a different
direction, the north east. These V-1s, it transpired, were being
launched from aircraft, a flight of about fifteen Heinkel 111s.
General Pile's AA promptly responded by moving some of
their guns to the East Anglian coast onto sites between
Clacton and Harwich. Shortly after this, Norfolk and Suffolk
were also on the receiving end of over forty V-2s aimed,
apparently, at the two big towns of Norwich and Ipswich, but
neither was hit.

In London the advent of the V-2 was once again
monitored by A P Herbert in his 'Doodlebug Log'. This
time, however, he was to have a much closer brush with
death when one of the rockets fell within a matter of yards
of his home. In the following extract, the novelist describes
his own experience as well as the prevailing feeling among
Londoners about what they were being told were a
succession of 'exploding gas-mains'!

In September the Canadians were storming along the coast of France, our doodlebug log was less busy, and we looked forward to an end of the Things. The last mentions of the V-1 I can find are for 18 September – 'Doodles – 2 or 3 – seemed to be coming from N.E.' (the Hague, I suppose), and 18 October – '1 Doodle'. '1 Doodle!' – poor little thing. But on 8 September we had begun to record 'Big Bangs', for a new plague had fallen on the patient Londoner – the V-2 rockets. These continued, off and on, for the next five months. Here, again, it seemed to me, the enemy did pretty good practice. The first one we heard in London fell in Grove Park, Chiswick, and the next at Chelsea, not very far from Westminster. The first 'bangs', it was whispered officially, were caused by exploding gas-mains or delayed-action bombs. Presently, so many gas-mains were exploding that it became a Metropolitan joke: but it was not till 2 January 1945 that the brutal word 'rocket' crept even into our confidential 'log'. Always, before that, it was 'bang' or 'big bang'.

The V-2, no doubt, was intended to be still more terrifying than the V-1, because there was no warning: but, for that very reason, I think, it was not. No warning is better than continual menace. You did not have to watch one across the sky and wonder where it would fall. There was a sudden bang, a slow column of smoke, and ruin in some small street: but, unless you were near that street, you forgot about it.

We were in dock for three weeks in the New Cross – Deptford area, where there were many, and some terrible, 'bangs'. But, even there, they were not always in the mind as the doodlebugs had been.

I did some more amateur map-work on the 'bangs', and I announced at last that our home at Hammersmith was 'on the main line' of the rockets. They came, I had heard, from somewhere near the Hague: and a line from the Hague to Westminster led on to the first 'gas-main' in Chiswick, I reckoned: and we were very near that line.

Sure enough, on the night of 1–2 January 1945, a rocket fell on the river bank, almost opposite, and less than 300 yards away. I had special leave to celebrate the thirtieth anniversary of our wedding: and friends had been singing round the piano by the front window till 0200. If it had fallen during the revels we should all have been cut to pieces: but it waited, fortunately, till 0340. The blast swept over the river, tore through the house (hardly touching our neighbours), and plucked great holes out of the roofs of the small houses behind us. But it did not even wake me. (I was sleeping at the back of the house, I should add, and my wife in the front: and they did say that the nearer you were to a rocket the less noise you heard.) I woke only when I heard my wife on the landing, saying calmly, 'Alan, come and look at me.' I went, wondering, and found her in a roomful of plaster and glass, but none the worse, thank God, and smiling still. Smiling, indeed: for, though we had seen many a nasty blitz through together on my leave-nights, it was an old joke that I was never there on the really big nights of Hammersmith and Hammersmith Terrace. Now, at last, there I was for our first rocket. All the windows and the frames as well were blown out for the fifth time. And I slept through it!

All I could say was: 'Well, I told you we were on the line.'

In the same week, I see, though our victorious troops were facing the Rhine, we recorded the fall of twenty rockets on London. But that was Hitler's last attempt upon my brave lady and her home – and about time too. She had had five and a half years of war and loneliness in London. She had had a bomb on the water at the end of the garden, and another, not far, on the other side of the house; two incendiaries on the roof and another (at the same time) in the front-room window by the hall. On that occasion, legend has it, a neighbour knocked on the door: my wife opened it with a charming smile, and said, 'It's all right. I know. The house is on fire.' She and two good neighbours put all three out.

She had had many a hair-raising ambulance drive through the black-out and the blitz, with screaming casualties behind her. When she was not doing that, or waiting for duty in a damp station with a glass roof, she was defending our tall house alone in the noisy night. Somehow, almost alone, she kept the house going all the war, dealt with my correspondence, grew vegetables for the King in the little flower-garden, and provided miraculous meals when hungry sailors appeared on leave. She lost all her windows time and again, and lived in the dark behind cardboard, or in the cold when the cardboard went. She would not go away, as many did: but stayed like a lighthouse of faith and fortitude among poorer neighbours who could not go. She had guarded a daughter, pregnant with twins, for four weeks of doodlebugs roaring over and falling not so far away.

And now, when surely the serious war is over at last, she celebrates her wedding-day, her ninth wedding-day in war-time, Fate sends a rocket, does its best to destroy her, and leaves her windowless in winter once again. And her husband sleeps. But still she smiled. And so did I. Of course we did. For how fortunate we were, after five and a half years, to be alive together in an old house still standing, on our ninth wedding-day at war! Still, I hope she has no more wedding-days at war, for she does not deserve it. No more, I know, gentlemen, do your heroic wives. I cannot tell their stories for you – but I salute them. It may be said that what they did and suffered is very small stuff beside the terrific tales of 'the few', the fighting men, the 'resistance' men, the prisoners, the spies – or beside the horrors of Hiroshima. But all these things were done and suffered by millions for a very long time: and it may be well to record them, for we forget so soon.

165

V-2 Blitz on London

It was not, in fact, until 9 November 1944 that the British Government finally admitted publicly that Hitler's new revenge weapon was being fired at England and only then after several devastating attacks on the metropolis.

Basil Collier has explained: 'In nine days at the end of October and early in November, forty-four rockets reached the country. Forty fell in the London Civil Defence Region or elsewhere within twenty-five miles of Charing Cross, and their mean point of impact was in Poplar, less than six miles east of the government quarter and at the heart of an important dockland area. Two rockets which fell at Camberwell and Deptford on 1 November killed or seriously injured more than 120 people. A week later the German authorities announced publicly that the V-2 offensive had begun.'

The German announcement was an almost exact repetition of the extravagant claims they had made for the V-1, and similarly the British media were quick to ridicule the boasts of Goebbels and his minions about 'the new blitz of London'. When Winston Churchill responded to these claims in the Houses of Parliament the following morning he deliberately did not mention London in connection with the attacks to withhold from the enemy any information about the targets the rockets were reaching. But there could still be no denying that the casualties at this time were as heavy as any during the war against the V-weapons.

The *Daily Express* gave up much of its front page of Thursday, 9 November to the revelations about the V-2, offering its readers details about the rocket which were in essence accurate, plus the first cut-away sketch of the missile. The story was written by staffman Basil Cardew who, in the months which followed, became regarded as the most informed writer on the V-2.

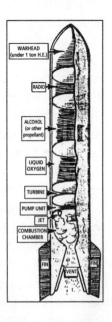

The Munich Beer Cellar Reunion, traditional holy day of the Nazi Party and the biggest of Germany's political galas, passed yesterday without a ceremony of any kind and without a word from the long-silent, mysteriously absent Adolf Hitler. Instead the people were bombarded with the message that a new secret weapon, the V-2, was now blitzing London.

It was the first time for 21 years that Hitler did not go to Munich for the anniversary of the Nazis' 1923 Putsch. In fact nothing came from him to break the silence he has kept since August soon after the bomb plot against him.

Last night the German News Agency said by way of

explanation, 'In this year of total war endeavour the traditional celebration will, for the first time, not be held in Munich.' For all that, earlier in the day the German censor had allowed neutral reporters in Berlin to cable, 'The party expects the Führer to make a speech.'

This political shock for the waiting Germany was covered up by a new development altogether, a sudden fanfare from Berlin radio about the V-2 weapon. Goebbels, by-passing Munich altogether, turned his full-blast propaganda flood on a story that for a month London had been bombarded by 'a terrible new weapon'.

All the German radio stations joined in the great radio blitz. Every Berlin paper front-paged V-2 claims in heavy type. V-2, they all proclaimed, was now in action successfully. The British government's silence on the matter helped to prove the devastating effect of the V-2.

The German High Command communiqué announcing the debut of the V-2 was repeated over and over again. But not a word was said to answer the question so often asked in the last three months: What has happened to Hitler?

If ever there was a logical and dramatic moment for him to break his silence, the Beer Cellar Day was the moment – and this one in particular for it would have marked the 'coming of age' of the abortive Nazi plot to seize Germany. And to make the point theatrically, the German radio was interrupted between seven and eight last night by a powerful ghost voice demanding repeatedly, 'Why does Hitler not speak? Where is Adolf Hitler?'

The radio, geared to the exultant new propaganda line, said nothing that gave a clue. On and on it repeated: 'The V-2 is in action. London is now being pounded with the greatest of secret weapons.'

The campaign began with a communiqué which said, 'For some weeks the attack on London has been intensified by the use of the new offensive weapon, V-2. The British Government has concealed from its people that a more effective, more telling and dangerous long-range weapon has been in action besides the flying bombs of which everyone knows by now.

'The German Command possess exact reports on the success and effect of the V-2. If they required further proof of the weapon's accuracy, official British reports have supplied it themselves. After nights in which London was exclusively attacked with V-2s, London announced that flying bombs had again been over the capital.

'For the time being nothing further can be made known about the technical details of this missile. According to reports from England, its characteristic feature is that it cannot be heard or perceived before its extraordinary heavy detonation. Reports speak of "unexplained explosions" and "extremely powerful blasts".

'The British Government is painfully endeavouring to prevent the population from hearing details of the V-2's explosive effect, and it is not allowing any reports of it to get abroad. Nevertheless, news that new explosive missiles of tremendous efficacy had hit London reached a neutral capital.

'Euston station was among the buildings completely destroyed in the middle of October. The London police ruthlessly made a cordon round the part of the town concerned and prevented sightseers from entering. Everybody involved was ordered to keep the strictest silence.

'Extremely heavy damage to blocks of houses and traffic installations is reported in Camberwell, Mitcham, Sidcup and Edmonton. A large railway bridge in South London was completely destroyed.

'Because of the V-2 the British Government was compelled to postpone the return of the evacuees to London. These are only a few of the reports about the success of the V-2 which, from now on, will carry out

German retaliation blows together with the V-1.'

The German radio network also broadcast the first eye-witness account by war reporter Hans Riecke, who said:

'About five months ago, the German High Command announcement on V-1 made the world stand by, exactly as it does today. Again the question of "What is the effect of the V-2?" is on everybody's lips. Let us remember how long it was before the world heard anything about the effectiveness of the V-1.

'The soldiers whom I have watched directing the V-2 against England may well be able to visualise the effects. But the enemy takes good care not to make the slightest mention of it. He does not say that his defences are able to deal with the V-2. He is just silent.

'The Fatherland's gratitude goes out to those research workers who, in spite of air terror, toiled untiringly, invented, tested, and developed the new weapon and eventually brought it into action. The soldiers and scientists using the V-2 can hit the enemy just where the High Command thinks fit.'

The German Overseas News Agency also brought its chief correspondent, Georg Schroeder, to sing the song of the V-2 last night. He said:

'Never before have the German military authorities been as reticent about secret weapons. Everybody in Germany now speaks about this secret weapon, but nobody knows anything definite. All the engineers and workers who have been mass-producing the V-2 are on their guard to give nothing away.

'The British hope that long-range fire on London would be stopped by the conquest of the Channel coast has not been fulfilled. How far are the launching sites of the V-2 from their targets? Is the V-2 a technical development of the V-1 or is it constructed according to a new principle? Military quarters give no reply. And the question of whether London and Southern England will remain the sole targets of the V-2 is also left unanswered in Berlin.'

Despite this German veil of secrecy, however, the V-2 is undoubtedly the weapon which Goebbels has been threatening will speedily end the war. It was first reported by American Army staff officers in Washington to have been used at Leningrad. It was then described as a giant rocket.

Warning that we might receive it came from Mr Churchill. Back in August he told the Commons that the enemy might launch long-range rocket shells with a heavier explosive force against us. He said London would probably be the primary target. Since then Mr Duncan Sandys, who was in charge of the counter-measures against the flying bomb, has said, 'I am a little chary of talking about the V-2, but we do know quite a lot about it.'

From information published in Sweden and other neutral countries it is possible today to give this unofficial description of the V-2:

It is a long, slim projectile, the shape of an ordinary shell. Its dimensions are between 30 and 50 feet in length and from five to seven feet in diameter. It weighs around 15 tons at the start and most of this is made up of fuel. The warhead does not exceed a ton of explosives.

The V-2 is fitted with several fins at the end. It is said to stand upright and be fired from a slab of concrete or an ordinary roadway. Its fuel is stated to be a combination of alcohol and liquid oxygen which is ignited on the ground until the thrust of escaping gas overcomes the weight of the rocket. Then it streaks into the air at enormous speed.

Stockholm reports also suggest that it is controlled probably by radio up to a height of 10 to 30 miles, when it is set on course. The angle at which it is then set is between 30 and 50 degrees according to the distance of the target.

THE FLYING BOMB WAR

Then, state the neutral informants, the V-2 climbs at a speed faster than sound to a height of 30 to 60 miles in the stratosphere. Its maximum speed at this height with little resistance from the air may reach 4,000 miles an hour. By then it is completely uncontrolled from the earth and follows a great arc-like course to its target.

On these facts, if reliable, it is reasonable to assume that its accuracy must be a matter of chance. Stockholm reports that the Germans have half a dozen sizes of this weapon. They may also be planning to use the atomic bomb in the warhead.

On the morning of Friday, 10 November, hard on the heels of all these newspaper stories about the Germans' wild claims for their new weapon – not to mention the talk of atom bombs – Winston Churchill stood up in the House of Commons to put the V-2 attacks into perspective. The speech which the Prime Minister gave is remembered as one of the most effective he delivered during the war: calming and reassuring, but none the less hinting that the Wellsian dream of a rocket capable of flying through space had now come true...

Last February, I told Parliament that the Germans were preparing to attack this country by means of long-range rockets, and I referred again to the possibility of this form of attack in my statement in this House on 6 July.

For the last few weeks the enemy has been using his new weapon, the long-range rocket, and a number have landed at widely scattered points in this country. In all, the casualties and damage have not so far been heavy, though I am sure the House would wish me to express our sympathy with the victims of these as of other attacks. No official statement about the attacks has hitherto been issued. The reason for this silence was that any announcement might have given information useful to the enemy, and we were confirmed in this course by the fact that, until two days ago, the enemy had made no mention of this weapon in his communiqués.

Last Wednesday an official announcement, followed by a number of highly coloured accounts of the attacks on this country, was issued by the German High Command. I do not propose to comment upon it except to say that the statements in this announcement are a good reflection of what the German Government would wish their people to believe, and of their desperate need to afford them some encouragement.

I may, however, mention a few facts. The rocket contains approximately the same quantity of high explosive as the flying bomb. However, it is designed to penetrate rather deeper before exploding. This results in somewhat heavier damage in the immediate vicinity of the crater, but rather less extensive blast effect around. The rocket flies through the stratosphere, going up to sixty or seventy miles, and outstrips sound. Because of its high speed, no reliable or sufficient public warning can, in present circumstances, be given.

There is, however, no need to exaggerate the danger. The scale and effects of the attack have not hitherto been significant. Some rockets have been fired at us from the island of Walcheren. This is now in our hands, and other areas from which rockets have, or can at present be fired against this country will, doubtless, be overrun by our Forces in due course. We cannot, however, be certain that the enemy will not be able to increase the range, either by reducing the weight of the warhead or by other methods. Nor, on the other hand, can we be certain that any new launching areas which he may establish further back will not, also in turn, be overrun by the advancing Allied Armies.

The use of this weapon is another attempt by the enemy to attack the morale of our civilian population in the vain hope that he may somehow by this means stave off the defeat which faces him in the field. Doubtless the enemy has hoped by his announcement to induce us to give him information which he has failed to get otherwise. I am sure that this House, the Press and the public will refuse to oblige him in this respect.

Spitfires Versus
the Rockets

Despite the fact that it was not until November that the general public were told officially about the V-2, efforts to try and counter them had already been going on for some time. Clearly the rockets were too fast and too unpredictable to be brought down by either fighter aircraft or AA guns and any balloon in the way of one of these mighty projectiles would be simply popped like a child's toy. If they could be stopped at all it would have to be at their point of departure. How the RAF responded, under the command of Air Chief Marshal Roderick Hill, who had been put in charge of co-ordinating offensive countermeasures against the long-range weapons almost immediately after the first salvo in early September, is here recounted by Hilary St George Saunders in an article he wrote for the American publication, *Life*, in April 1945. Saunders, who was later to write the definitive three-volume history of the RAF in World War II, reveals the part played by the versatile Spitfire in achieving another victory for the nation as vital in many ways as its contribution to the Battle of Britain.

The Spitfire which played such a significant role as a fighter aircraft in the Battle of Britain was called upon to fulfil an entirely new role in the battle against the V-2 rockets which began in the autumn of 1944. The latest Spitfire, the Mark XVI, was used not for aerial combat but as a bomber to drop explosives on the launching sites of the missiles in Holland, many of which were located on The Hague in densely wooded areas or in the shadows of civilian buildings.

Following the opening of the V-2 campaign against England in September, a drizzle of rockets fell on Southern England throughout the next two months, and RAF Fighter Command and the American Tactical Air Force were ordered to conduct an offensive against the area lying between The Hague and Leiden and in the neighbourhood of the Hook of Holland. The experts believed that it was from here that most of the rockets were being launched, although the exact location was not known.

Between 15 October and 25 November, the Second Tactical Air Force flew nearly 10,000 sorties and Fighter Command over 600, during the course of which much German transport was destroyed, but it was impossible to discover whether the activities of the crews firing the rockets had been affected.

As the casualties from the rocket attacks continued to mount in England – culminating on 25 November when a rocket landed in New Cross, Deptford killing over 160 people – the British Government's natural reluctance to bomb a crowded city like The Hague in the far from certain hope that the crews launching the weapons, or the weapons themselves, might be destroyed, gradually lessened. Their decision on a future course of action was then made easier by members of the Dutch Government in London who felt that if such attacks were likely to prove successful, they should be made.

Coincidental with the tragedy at New Cross, the RAF announced that the aircraft of No. 12 Group, which consisted largely of Spitfires, were to be turned into bombers. It was believed that the highly flexible, adaptable and deadly Mark XVI would be ideal for

attacking the small and difficult targets of the rocket
sites.

These bomber-Spitfires, it was revealed, had already
made a successful attack on 21 November on a V-2
storage, erection and launching installation in a Dutch
wood where a rocket was actually waiting to be fired.
Bombs which hit the installations and strikes of
strafing on the rocket itself were the measure of the
day's success, it was stated.

An unnamed pilot who took part in this mission and
in several which followed said afterwards, 'The sites are
very difficult to locate, but once we have found one we
try to approach in a power dive from about 8,000 feet
through cloud gaps. It is necessary to fly very low over
the sites – often close to tree-top level – letting fly with
our guns as we go in. Then we try to plant our two
250lb bombs with 11-second delayed action fuses right
on the target. After that we climb over the trees and get
away as quickly as possible!'

These Spitfire assaults were aimed at eleven targets
in all, seven of them in the densely wooded areas of The
Hague. The other four were suspected storage areas at
Wassenaar, at Voorde and Huis ten Werve, and the
Hotel Promenade at The Hague which was believed to
be housing rocket-firing troops.

Although there were those in the British Government at this time, including the Home Secretary, who
continued to press for stronger countermeasures
against the rockets – fearing that they might be able to
penetrate the Tube stations, in which many people
were sheltering, with a consequent heavy loss of life –
the decision prevailed that to use heavy bombers would
be to destroy much Dutch property without achieving
any conclusive results.

So the Spitfire-bombers continued their fast and
precise attacks throughout the daylight hours of the
winter, often in appalling weather. At this same time,

other fighter patrols were also making attacks on the supply lines of rail or road leading to the Serderger-stadtschutzplatz, as the Germans called their rocket-launching sites.

Despite the bad weather which caused a high proportion of the sorties to be abandoned, some notable successes were achieved. In one five-day period, for example, more than twenty-five separate attacks were made, all in the face of intense anti-aircraft defences.

On Christmas Eve, thirty-three of the Mark XVI Spitfires carried out the heaviest single attack yet mounted on a block of flats at Marlot near the Haagsche Bosch, which was believed to be the headquarters of the rocket-firing troops in the vicinity. Each of the Spitfires of Numbers 229 and 602 Squadrons and Number 453 of the Royal Australian Air Force – carrying one 500lb and two 250lb bombs apiece – inflicted considerable damage on the flats and caused the building to be evacuated.

Weeks of special training had, of course, been necessary to prepare these Spitfire bomber pilots for their exacting task, and their dedication was marked by some spectacular achievements. When a rocket store and firing installation was spotted within 300 yards of the historic Dutch Royal Palace, Huis ten Bosch, for instance, the danger to this important historical building was obvious. But members of the 453 Squadron RAAF put their bombs right on the target in a single attack. Similarly, when the Germans installed V-2 equipment in the grounds of a hotel and ran a railway siding into a narrow gully between a housing estate and a hospital, the Spitfires again bombed the site including the trains and the rocket, but left the houses and hospital unharmed.

Although it has to be said that these Spitfire attacks were largely ineffective in stopping the V-2, they were the only riposte that the Royal Air Force, or indeed the Armed Forces in general, could make at this time against a weapon which, could it have been controlled with accuracy, might have inflicted the gravest damage.

The assaults on the wooded areas continued, however, with what result it was almost impossible to say. On occasions the dropping of a bomb or burst of cannon fire would be followed by a heavy explosion which seemed to indicate that a rocket had been hit, but the general results must be described as meagre. Nevertheless, the number of rockets reaching London remained few, only 57 falling in the first half of December as against 86 in the previous fortnight. There were, though, at this time two serious incidents in which a total of 107 people were killed and 134 injured, one in Islington and the other at Chelmsford.

The reason for this slackening of the enemy's efforts against London was, in all probability, because he increased them against Antwerp, which received 217 rockets during the period when von Rundstedt was conducting the last desperate offensive of the Wehrmacht through the Ardennes. As soon as this was over, the weekly average of rockets falling in the United Kingdom rose from 34 in December to 59 in January.

The attacks of the Spitfire fighter-bombers had at least had the effect of inducing the Germans to fire the rockets at night rather than during the day. And warning of the advent of rockets was also slowly improving, largely through the activities of No. 105 Mobile Air Reporting Unit at Malines in Belgium which was able to monitor the launching of V-2s and report the fact to England.

As the year drew to a close, however, repeated examination and analysis of the rocket-bomb attacks forced upon the authorities the melancholy conclusion that only between 4 and 15 December when it had been possible to maintain the Spitfire fighter-bomber attacks on The Hague on a reasonably large scale, had the volume of German fire been reduced. Obviously new tactics were required if the weapon, like the war itself, was to be successfully curtailed in 1945.

The V-2 rocket mentioned by Hilary St George Saunders which fell on New Cross on 25 November with such terrible consequences received hardly a line in the national press the following morning, despite the fact that all the newspapers sent reporters to the scene. Indeed, because of the reporting restrictions then in force, the following account of the tragedy which Basil Cardew wrote for the *Daily Express* remained on file for five months before it finally appeared, slightly revised, in print.

The most vicious blow struck by the V-2 rockets occurred on a Saturday morning in November in the High Street at New Cross. What happened that day was the second worst bomb disaster of the entire war.

The people of New Cross were doing their weekend shopping. Mothers had brought their children with them who were home from school for the morning. Some of them were buying little presents in advance for Christmas.

Local gossip had been busy that morning, The news had got around that a consignment of kitchen buckets had reached a store in the High Street. Already there was a queue of women shoppers to buy them.

It was also said that there was fish to be had in a nearby shop and this had created a second queue. A third line of women was also to be seen outside a draper's shop which was about to put on sale some much sought-after bed sheets.

It was at ten past twelve that New Cross earned a place in history: a place it would doubtless rather not have had, but will surely retain forever. There was not a sound of warning. And in an instant, Hitler's deathblow had converted the busy, homely scene to a shambles.

So great was the force of the explosion that the whole

of the store – with all the people in it, shoppers and staff alike – was thrown into the basement, with hundreds of tons of masonry, splintered timbers and twisted steel girders above them.

Within one and a half minutes of the V-2's arrival, however, rescue squads were at work. Brick by brick the debris was removed by hand by the rescuers. Shattered bodies, some of them children still clasping the toys that had been bought for them only a few moments earlier, were uncovered and tenderly removed.

Between 70 and 80 bodies were recovered from Woolworths alone. Of eleven others no trace has been found to this day. Five minutes before the V-2 fell, a woman named Mrs Peaves had left her sister and baby in the store. Neither has been traced. Another woman found her husband's van 'crushed like a concertina' just outside – but of her husband there was no trace.

On that terrible morning when the V-2 fell, 168 men, women and children fell in action. A further 108 were seriously injured. It required every ounce of English resilience for the people of New Cross to get on with their lives – and to laugh at that old joke that it had been another of those 'gas-main explosions'.

Christmas Mail
by Flying Bomb!

On Christmas Eve, Sunday, 24 December, there was a dramatic change in the Germans' tactics with the V-1s. Instead of directing the flying bombs at London from the remaining launching sites across the North Sea and occasionally from the air, a force of fifty Heinkel aircraft each carrying a V-1 slung under its belly this time flew to a point just off the east coast between Skegness and Bridlington and launched their charges in the direction of... Manchester. These V-1s were also unusual in that they were carrying copies of letters from British prisoners of war and bundles of propaganda material! The items were carried in containers which were released just before the flying bombs made their final dive, and they fell to the ground like a sprinkling of snow just as Christmas morning dawned.

Not surprisingly, neither the intended target of these raiders nor the 'Christmas Mail' they were carrying was mentioned in the newspaper reports of the attack which appeared immediately after Christmas. The *Daily Sketch* of 27 December was typical of most papers with its story.

For the first time flying bombs were launched against targets in northern England. The attack was widespread and guns and fighters went into action. Several successes are believed to have been registered.

Previously only southern England has been the goal for airborne V-bombs. This new line of attack may indicate that the German Air Force leaders are tiring of attacking the south because the defences have achieved such a high percentage of success. It is unlikely, however, that the attacks will be stepped up to the old proportions since the Germans have only a limited number of planes able to carry the bombs.

(As a matter of record, only 18 of these flying bombs got within a range of 15 miles of the centre of Manchester, while 37 people were killed and 67 seriously injured.)

Although literally dozens of people picked up the letters and propaganda sheets, their existence remained another closely guarded secret until after the war. The letters were printed in black and red on a small sheet headed: V-1 POW POST. Each contained facsimiles of letters from prisoners whose homes were in the north of England. Beneath these was an appeal which read: 'The finder is requested to cut out or copy the letters printed here and to transmit them to the addresses so that they receive them as early as possible. The original letters are being sent through the Red Cross Mail in the usual channel.' The intention of the letters was transparently obvious – the Germans hoped that a relative might reply to a POW mentioning the location in which the letter – and by inference the flying bomb – had landed. Fortunately, the police acted quickly to collect this illicit mail, and although it was later decided that the letters should be forwarded to their intended recipients, these people were warned not to mention in any reply that they had received them.

Also dropped by the flying bombs were copies of a German propaganda sheet entitled *The Other Side* which were similarly quickly gathered up by the authorities to prevent any information getting back to the enemy as to where they had landed. An example of one of these unique Christmas missives has, fortunately, survived and the text is reprinted hereunder. Its tone is a fascinating reminder of what was to prove the Germans' last desperate attempt to cause alarm and despondency through the medium of the flying bomb – for very few more V-1s were launched from the air, the final one landing in Hornsey, London on 14 January 1945.

THE OTHER SIDE
V-1: Those 'Last Few Shots'!

Since May 1943 the RAF have been bombing the invulnerable factories of Hitler's secret weapon. But you were not told a word about it in the press.

You were told – remember? – that this secret weapon was just a bluff. Just German propaganda. It was only Germany trying to whip up fresh quarrels. Britain, you were also told, had nothing to fear from any so-called secret weapons.

Then the V-1 came.

We don't have to tell you or to describe the terror it caused. You have seen the results for yourselves. That was the first part of what you were not supposed to know.

Churchill has dismissed the facts of this evidence. He has claimed that the RAF have been successful in destroying the sites from which the secret weapons are launched.

Yet the V-1s keep coming. And now German scientists have invented a new and still more destructive weapon.

It is the V-2.

The RAF will have to start all over again. And what you will be told about this new weapon will be wrong again.

It is time for the British people to listen to the words of reason of the Führer. Give up this war – it is one you cannot hope to win.

The message was obviously intended to make the flesh of

British readers creep. For good measure the Germans even included 'The V Puzzle', a crossword puzzle with the black squares placed so as to make a V-1 design!

Clues across: 1. He is your enemy, too. 7. V-1 is so fast, that it is hard to this. 8. Partly a beverage. 10. This is the beginning of a German victory. 11. We hear that this is a rare commodity in England. 13. This is in Latin. 14. He wants all you've got.

Down: 1. In the case of the air war, he has been bit by V-1. 2. Money but no pence. 3. Men and material intended for Normandy very often finish at the bottom of this. 4. V-1 contains this. 5. Britain has none at inter-Allied conferences. 6. At Tehran, Churchill practically did this before Stalin. 9. First person singular. 10. Two reprisals with nothing in between. 12. Warmongers must this, if England is to be saved. 13. That man.

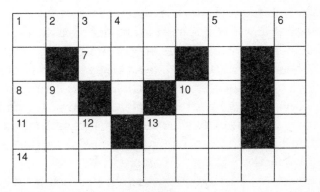

V-1 is a puzzle for the British Government, and this puzzle is in the form of V-1. If you choose to regard the cross-word merely as an entertainment, no doubt you will get some fun out of it. If you take it seriously you will get more than that – you will find that it contains some very useful advice!

There is a curious 'prequel' to this story to be found in the pages of *Hansard*, the daily report of the proceedings of the Houses of Parliament, for Friday, 30 June 1944 when the Conservative MP for Chatham, Captain Leonard Plugge, asked whether any thought had been given to flying bombs being used as mail carriers. Captain Plugge was no wild-eyed eccentric, but a man with a life-long interest in aeronautics, having served in the RAF as a captain during World War I, and then worked at both the Royal Aircraft Establishment at Farnborough and the Department of Scientific Research at the Air Ministry before becoming an MP in 1935. At the time he rose to speak in the Chamber he was also chairman of the Parliamentary Science Committee. The exchange between him and the Under Secretary of State for Air is reported by *Hansard* in these words:

CAPTAIN PLUGGE (Chatham, U) asked the Secretary of State for Air whether the pilotless plane was being considered in connection with post-war activities; and whether plans were being made for developing it for the purpose of dispatching mail over long distances at high speed at frequent intervals on regular routes.

CAPTAIN BALFOUR, Under Secretary of State for Air (Isle of Thanet, U) replied that pilotless aircraft had been developed some years before the war for certain purposes. Possibilities for such aircraft for commercial use, including the carriage of mail, have certainly not been overlooked by my department, he said.

CAPTAIN PLUGGE asked if in view of the knowledge we had acquired in the meantime, the Ministry would consult with the Postmaster General on the possibility of experimenting with the carriage of mail in this manner?

CAPTAIN BALFOUR: 'I think there is some confusion in the mind of my Hon. Friend. Flying bombs of the kind used by the enemy are an entirely different proposition. They are not expected to land safely at a particular destination (laughter) and they cannot be used more than once (again laughter). Commercial aircraft we expect to land safely at their expected destination and we expect to use them repeatedly.' (Laughter and repeated cheers.)

Joking apart, here was evidence that some people were already anticipating future uses for flying bombs no sooner than they had seen them. And with the ultimate evolution of the V2 into a rocket capable of carrying men – as well as mail, if so required – around the world and into space, perhaps it might be said that Captain Plugge had the last laugh after all!

Silencing the
'Big Bens'

As the year 1945 dawned, so the anxiety about the V-2 increased. More detailed reports of the casualties and destruction caused by these missiles were now appearing in the national newspapers, although editors were still carefully following Churchill's instructions not to be any more specific about the locations than 'southern England'. To the people of London who were feeling the weight of these attacks, however, such a deception was little compensation for all the pain they were going through. The man charged with countering the V-2, Air Chief Marshal Sir Roderick Hill, was well aware of this suffering and early in January redoubled his efforts and introduced new tactics as he explains in the following article which he wrote for the *London Gazette* in October 1945. Hill brought a special dedication to his task for not only had he flown against the flying bombs the previous summer but also enjoyed the satisfaction of shooting one 'Diver' down while he was on patrol on the approaches to London. Now he had his sights firmly set on silencing the 'Big Bens' once and for all...

In the New Year the scale of V-2 attacks went up again. During the first half of January an average of more than eight rockets a day reached this country. Thereafter the rate of fire declined a little, only to rise again early in February, until an average of ten rockets a day was attained in the middle of the month. Moreover, the Germans again took to doing more than half their firing in daylight, and their accuracy improved. In an average week in January and the first half of February, twice as many people were killed or seriously injured by rockets as in a corresponding period in December.

Clearly, our fighter-bomber programme was not such an effective deterrent as we had hoped. This was not to say that our methods were wrong: without the fighter-bomber attacks, the rate of fire might have risen still more sharply. But evidently something more was needed if the German offensive was to be kept down.

What form that something more should take was not so obvious. In December the Air Ministry had asked the Foreign Office and the Ministry of Economic Warfare to investigate the possibility of curtailing supplies of fuel for the A-4 by attacking factories where liquid oxygen was made. The experts reported that there was no means of knowing which of the many factories in German hands or under German control were supplying liquid oxygen for that particular purpose. There were, however, eight factories in Holland, five in western Germany, and five elsewhere in Germany which might fill the bill.

As a sequel to this investigation, the Air Ministry invited me to consider attacking three factories in Holland. One of them, at Alblasserdam, near Dordrecht, was successfully attacked by the Second Tactical Air Force on 22 January. Another, at Ijmuiden, consisted of two buildings so closely surrounded by other factories that the prospect of a successful attack with the means at my disposal was remote. The third, at Loosduinen, on the outskirts of the Hague, was adjoined on three sides by Dutch civilian property. Hence I was reluctant to attack it, especially as there was no certainty that its destruction would cause the Germans to fire even one less rocket at this country.

However, in view of the Air Ministry's request and my desire to leave nothing undone which offered a chance of hampering the enemy, I agreed to do so. In order to reduce the risk to civilian property to a minimum, the pilots chosen for the job were instructed to use methods which can best be described as 'trickling their bombs towards the target'. This technique necessitated five separate attacks of which all but one were made from the direction in which there were no houses adjoining the factory. Two attacks were made on 3 February, two on 9 February, and one on the 8th. After the last attack on the 9th we judged that the target had suffered enough damage to be left alone in future.

In January bad weather limited the number of fighter-bomber sorties that we could make to a little more than half the number made in December. In February the weather was better and during the first half of the month we made more fighter-bomber sorties than in the whole of January. Besides delivering the five attacks on the oxygen factory at Loosduinen to which I have alluded, we made six attacks on the Haagsche Bosch, a wooded area in which rockets had been seen on reconnaissance photographs taken in December. The Hotel Promenade was attacked on three occasions, and attacks were also made on other suspected storage areas at the Hague, Wassenaar, and the Hook of Holland, as well as on railway targets. The Second Tactical Air Force continued to attack communications, as hitherto, in the course of their armed reconnaissance and rail interdiction programmes.

Meanwhile, in consequence of the rise in the scale of rocket attack, towards the end of January the Air Ministry had begun to press me to intensify my efforts against the firing and storage areas. Nevertheless they were still unwilling to see any part of Bomber Command's effort diverted to the attack of such targets. On the 26th of the month, however, the

Defence Committee agreed to invite the Air Ministry to ask Supreme Headquarters to sanction the precise attacks on selected targets by the light bombers of No. 2 Group, which I had been urging since the previous autumn. Shortly before this I had arranged to raise the strength of the force earmarked for exclusive use against rocket targets from four squadrons to six, and to equip and use all six squadrons regularly as fighter-bomber squadrons. (The additional squadrons selected were Nos. 451 (Spitfire XVI) and 124 (Spitfire IX, modified for bombing).)

I now negotiated a new agreement with the Second Tactical Air Force whereby my area of responsibility was extended as far east as Amersfoort. On days when the weather was unsuitable for precise attack on objectives at the Hague, our fighter-bombers were now attacking rail targets; and the inclusion of Amersfoort in our area would enable us to bomb the railway junction there – a bottleneck through which all traffic from Germany to the firing areas in western Holland passed. Under the terms of the new agreement the Second Tactical Air Force would use any light or medium bombers that they could spare from the battle on land to attack rocket targets chosen from lists provided by my staff.

The full effect of the expansion of the 'Big Ben' fighter-bomber force was seen in the second half of February, when Fighter Command made 548 sorties and dropped 108 tons of bombs – precisely the same weight in two weeks as in the previous six. At the suggestion of my Chief Intelligence Officer, who recommended that we should try the effect of concentrating our efforts on a single target for at least a week, nearly three-quarters of this bomb tonnage was aimed at the Haagsche Bosch, where severe damage was done, particularly on 22 February, when a film studio which the Germans used for storage was gutted.

An almost complete cessation of rocket fire over a period of more than sixty hours followed this attack; and on 24 February photographic reconnaissance failed to reveal a single rocket anywhere in the square mile or so of wooded parkland that the Haagsche Bosch comprised. Other evidence strengthened the inference that the Germans had been driven from the Haagsche Bosch, at least for the time being, and suggested that they had been forced to improvise facilities in the racecourse area at Duindigt, further to the north.

So far as they went, these results of our new policy of concentrating on one area were encouraging; but events soon showed that no lasting effect on the Germans had been achieved. When firing was resumed (apparently from Duindigt) on the 26th, no appreciable decline in its quality or quantity was apparent. Nor did the first of No. 2 Group's long-awaited bombing attacks, which was delivered on 3 March, have any better effect. The attack was delivered by 56 Mitchells, and the target chosen – not without some misgivings since the continued presence of the Germans and their gear was doubtful – was the Haagsche Bosch. Unfortunately the bombing was not sufficiently accurate, in consequence of which casualties occurred among Dutch civilians and their property was damaged. After this unhappy experience, Air Marshal Coningham decided to make no more attacks on targets at the Hague.

Another countermeasure considered at this stage was the use of anti-aircraft artillery to fire at approaching rockets and explode them in the air. If only because the rockets travelled many times faster than the fastest bomber and completed their parabolic flight from Holland in less than five minutes, the problems involved seemed formidable. Indeed, proposals in this sense had been carefully considered before the attacks began and found impracticable. General Pile raised the subject again in December, 1944, when he asked permission to make an operational trial of a scheme designed to ensure that the rockets would pass through a curtain of shell-fragments as they approached the earth. An essential requirement of the plan was accurate and timely warning that a rocket was on its way. Although there were still difficulties in the way of disseminating such warnings to the public, for operational purposes reliable information of this kind was now available. There were some obvious drawbacks to the scheme: for example, the expenditure of rounds required to explode even one rocket was likely to be extravagant and possibly alarming to the public.

Nevertheless, I was satisfied that it contained the germ of a successful countermeasure, which might become important in the future, and that on purely operational grounds a practical trial was desirable. I made recommendations to this effect when submitting General Pile's proposal to higher authority. The committee before whom the scheme was laid, after taking the opinion of eminent men of science, one of whom put the chances of a successful engagement at one in a hundred and another at one in a thousand, decided that an operational trial would be premature. They invited those concerned to seek ways of improving the scheme, and promised to consider it again in March.

Accordingly General Pile repeated his request for an operational trial towards the end of that month. He pointed out that time was clearly running out: the opportunity of testing the scheme in practice would soon have passed. In response, on 26 March a panel of scientists were asked to prepare a theoretical estimate of success. They reported on the same day that if 400 rounds were fired against any one rocket the chance of scoring a hit would, at best, be one in thirty. After a further statement by General Pile, who said that he would endeavour to increase the chance of success by trebling the rate of fire, the proposal went before the Chiefs of Staff, who decided on 30 March that the likelihood of success was too small to outweigh the objections to the scheme. But in any case, by that time the campaign was over.

Meanwhile we had been continuing our fighter-bomber offensive against the rocket-firing organisation and its communications. After 3 March we made no further attacks on the Haagsche Bosch, but turned our attention to the adjoining racecourse area at Duindigt, along with other storage and firing areas and a group of buildings belonging to the Bataafsche Petroleum Company, which apparently the Germans were using as billets and offices. As before, we selected railway targets for attack when conditions were unsuitable for attacking our primary objectives. During the second week of March alone we dropped some 70 tons of bombs at Duindigt. By the middle of the month we had evidence that the Germans had abandoned the area, which was by that time so pitted with craters that, in the words of a contemporary report, 'it looked as if Bomber Command, not Fighter Command, had been attacking it'.

This success was accompanied by another temporary decrease in the scale of rocket attack on London; and what was, perhaps, more significant was that about this time the Germans took to doing more and more of their firing in the early hours before dawn. We concluded that our efforts had spoilt their arrangements for storing rockets in the forward area and that they were being forced to bring the missiles up at night and fire them off as soon as possible. Accordingly, during the second half of March we paid little attention to storage areas and devoted most of our fighter-bomber effort to communications. Altogether we made more fighter-bomber sorties in March than in the previous four months put together, and dropped more than three times the weight of bombs dropped in February.

The German offensive came to an end at 1645 hours on 27 March, when the one thousand, one hundred and fifteenth rocket to fall in this country or within sight of shore fell to earth at Orpington, in Kent. The campaign had lasted seven months. During that time the Germans had fired at least 1,300 rockets at London and some 40 or more at Norwich. Of these 518 had fallen within the London Civil Defence Region and none at all within the boundaries of the latter city. Altogether, 2,511 people had been killed and 5,869 seriously injured in London, and 213 killed and 598 seriously injured elsewhere.

These figures would have been substantially smaller but for a number of unlucky incidents, in which rockets chanced to hit crowded buildings. Among the worst of these incidents were three which occurred at New Cross Road, Deptford, on 25 November, 1944, and at Smithfield Market and Hughes Mansions, Stepney, on 8 and 27 March respectively. Deplorable as these occurrences were, their rarity is a measure of the random quality of the long-range rocket in the stage to which the Germans had developed it.

Yet the rocket cannot be dismissed as a mere freak. Practically, it was a new weapon, which brought new hazards to the lives of millions, and set new problems of defence. Its significance, and that of the flying bomb, when posed against the wider background of the war as a whole, remain to be considered.

Air Chief Marshal Hill had not been the only service chief worried about the potential of German rocket weapons at the start of 1945. There was also a fear among certain senior American forces' leaders that the United States could well be in the range of the flying bombs and might be next to feel their impact, as the following report from the *Daily Telegraph* of Tuesday 9 January indicates:

ROBOTS MAY HIT NEW YORK

'Robot rocket raids against New York and the East Coast of America are possible and probable within the next 30 or 60 days,' Admiral Ingram, Commander-in-Chief United States Atlantic Fleet declared today. 'If such an attempt is made it will probably be limited to 10 or 12 bombs, but I have moved plenty of forces in readiness and the next Alert will be the real thing.'

The Admiral, who revealed that he was taking over the coastal defences of New York and Washington, issued the warning at a press conference aboard his flagship at an East Coast port. He said he had been authorised to do so by Admiral King, C-in-C, United States Fleet.

Stating that he had had a series of important conferences with officers of all the military defence units along the East Coast, Admiral Ingram continued:

'There is no reason for anyone to become alarmed. The Army and Navy are well prepared to ward off any attacks. Adequate protective measures have been taken. I don't think measures were adequate earlier.

'If the Germans attempt to send robot bombs against New York or Washington, the weapons will hardly be of the block-buster type used against London because they will carry more fuel and have less explosive. They might strike a building and destroy it, but casualties would be nothing like those the people of London have been suffering. The greatest danger would be from fires, but panic could increase the danger.'

Admiral Ingram said that there were three possible ways by which robot bombs could be launched: from long-range planes, submarines or surface ships. The Atlantic was under 'mighty fine protection' against surface ship approach, he said.

The danger area was a 300-mile arc in which New York and Washington might be hit, though the Germans might get as close as 200 miles of New York.

'They might try to hit the Empire State Building to cause a panic,' Admiral Ingram said. 'It is difficult to stop a robot attack unless we catch it at source. Regardless of air coverage in this area I think bombs could get through.

'But let them come – we are ready to meet the situation. I will catch everything coming from Europe without a glove. The Germans have at least 300 U-boats in the Atlantic. The Navy is prepared to keep them from coming close enough to fire, or to stop them before they have fired many bombs. Six to eight U-boats would be needed to attack New York.'

Asked if his visit to the port was due to the possibility of robot bomb attacks, Admiral Ingram agreed it was. He said he could not disclose the steps taken to meet such a possible attack on New York. Such an attack would naturally be welcomed for political purposes by Goebbels.

'As for the U-boats,' he concluded, 'they are no longer much of a menace. I cannot reveal the weapons we have used, or when and where, or how many submarines have been sunk.'

Colonel E. Thomas, the Director of the New York State Office of Civilian Protection, also issued a bulletin to officials stating: 'The possibilities of extensive robot bomb attacks on New York are slight. Possible damage and destruction will not be concentrated or continuous. No complete black-out would be ordered in case of an attack as it would be detrimental to rescue and salvage operations.'

This statement, combined with Admiral Ingram's warning, has brought about a profound change in the attitude of many New Yorkers who had thought all talk of possible raids was 'alarmist nonsense'.

The Day I Survived a V-2

On the morning of Friday, 16 March 1945 *The Times* carried an announcement which read: 'London can now be named as the target of V-2 rocket attacks. Hitherto the term "southern England" has been used.' This inevitable decision may well have been reached because of the appalling death toll caused by a rocket which had fallen on Smithfield on 8 March killing or seriously injuring 233 people and which had become common gossip all over the Eastern Counties, such were the numbers of people coming and going from this important market centre. But as events were to prove, the decision was almost unnecessary for the V-2 was soon to be no more...

The article in *The Times* continued:

> Under these attacks the capital has carried on as usual, as it did through the Blitz and through the flying-bomb onslaught. Attendances at amusements have shown no decline. Night life in the West End has not been interrupted. Football crowds, particularly the Cup matches, have reached almost peace-time figures. Life in London has gone on despite the V-2 attacks.

Among the millions of Londoners going on with their lives that day was young Hazel Cooper of Woolwich, who now lives in Welling, Kent and maintains a keen interest in history, especially that of the Second World War which so shaped her own life. Indeed, the very day after that announcement in *The Times*, Mrs Cooper made a little piece of history herself when she survived what was to prove one of the last V-2s to hit London. She made contact with me after a radio broadcast in which I asked listeners for personal stories about the V-2. This is her moving story told in her own words.

One of the very last V-2 rockets to fall on England landed close to where I lived in Jackson Street, Woolwich. It happened at about 8 a.m. on 17 March 1945, and killed fourteen of our very dear friends and neighbours, including my best friend, Audrey Deer, with whom I used to go to the Girl Guides each week.

I was eleven years old at the time and my memories of the events of that day are very clear. Yet it could so easily have been a quite different story, because earlier that year I and my sister, Joyce, who was three years younger than me, had been evacuated from London to Bradford, Yorkshire.

Unlike a lot of other people who were very happy in their new homes, my sister and I were very homesick for Woolwich. All the more so when my aunt who was still living in Woolwich wrote to tell us that nothing much was happening there.

So my mother decided to take a chance and took us back to Jackson Street and we were in our little home once again when the V-2 rocket fell on that Saturday morning.

I know looking back that we behaved rather foolishly – but at the time the rocket fell we had got rather brave and instead of sleeping in the Anderson shelter in the garden as we should have done, we preferred to sleep downstairs in the house. For despite the fact that a number of doodlebugs had already fallen at Woolwich we thought the Germans were after the Army Barracks on Woolwich Common.

I remember one of the doodlebugs actually hit

Butter's Dairy which was just around the corner from where we lived, but we all thought they were not as bad as the rockets because you could hear them coming and run for cover.

With the V-2, of course, we had no warning. It was the worst experience of my life and something I have not forgotten in sixty years.

My sister and I had just woken up and were still in our nighties in our bedroom. Then there was this eerie sound, which we realised later was the rocket, followed by a terrible explosion outside. The blast seemed to go in a funny way as it came down the road, turning round to the back of our house and saving us from death.

Then there was a pause and everything was absolutely quiet for several seconds. After that all you could hear were people screaming from their terrible injuries, followed by the arrival of the firemen and Army personnel to rescue us. They were wonderful!

The blast had rocked our room and shattered a photograph frame that was hanging on the wall. My sister and I were injured by flying glass splinters and were both very shocked.

At the time, I was playing with a Hungarian doll that had been given to me by a young actress called Billie Whitelaw. She had been a friend of an Army major my father had known when we were stationed at Aberystwyth before the war started.

Billie and her family had invited us to tea and she had given me the doll as a present. It was very precious to me and I was heartbroken when I lost it as a result of that V-2. In fact, it was the thing that most upset me that day!

Our mother, though, was much worse injured than Joyce and I and she had to be rushed off to the hospital at Shooters Hill for treatment to her head injuries.

The next thing I remember were soldiers from the barracks arriving to help get us out from the debris. We looked awful with black and dust all over us, and, of course, we were still in our nighties!

I remember standing out in the street for quite a long time watching our next-door neighbour being dug out of the ruins of her house. She was 72 years old.

'What the bloody hell was that?' were the first words I heard her say to one of her rescuers.

The vans of the WVS were also on the scene very quickly and they gave us tea to drink for the shock and also buns to eat.

There are other memories I will never forget of things which occurred during that day before Joyce and I were taken to Eglington School, which we both attended, to spend the night, because our house was obviously unsafe to go back to.

I remember there were a couple who lived in our road who were found dead in each other's arms. They were newlyweds. Then there was my little friend, Audrey Deer, whose home suffered a direct hit from the rocket. They were only able to identify her body by the little ring on one of her fingers. And all they could find of her little pet dog who was always by her side were a few bits of bones.

When my father, who was away serving with the Army abroad, heard the news of the rocket landing on Jackson Street he was furious. He said we should not have come back home. But he was very happy when my mother recovered in hospital and we were all reunited.

I learned later that 36 houses in Jackson Street and Milward Street were wholly or substantially damaged on that Saturday morning. Our local paper, the *Kentish Independent* said that the explosion of the rocket caused 'a scene of widespread havoc in a mass of rubble with clouds of dust rising over the area'.

In fact, the damage caused by that V-2 merged with the earlier devastation of the Blitz and the various V-1 incidents so that the turnings such as Jackson Street,

Milward Street, Engineer Street and Gildersome Street vanished from the map of Woolwich. Our home could not be rebuilt and we were later housed in a prefab. Of those streets where I grew up, only a few are remembered today in names to be found in the modern residential estate which now occupies the area.

It was a miracle that the three of us in that house in Jackson Street were not killed and that's why I'm so grateful for every year of my life. This anniversary makes me forgive but never forget what I experienced. I would never want any of my family to go through those awful days.

My cousin, Emily Page, who also survived that same V-2 rocket, wrote her memories of the event a little while later and I should like to add them to my own. The aunt and her two children whom she refers to are my mother, my sister and me...

'It all happened very suddenly, without a sound or warning. I was still in bed on the ground floor of our house, my little daughter, Vivien, who was two years old, also in bed with me. Being in bed that morning probably saved our lives.

'I became aware that something terrible had happened when the ceiling began to come down on us and the walls came caving in. I remember having difficulty in breathing because of all the dust and my first thoughts were to cover my little girl with my body. The bedclothes helped to protect us from the falling ceiling.

'There was not a sound at this time, but after a while I could hear screams of help from my immediate neighbours. When I recovered from the shock I scrambled out of bed with my daughter in my arms and made my way to the kitchen over all the debris. I just stood there thinking to myself, "I must make a cup of tea"!

'After a short while I heard voices and a fireman and

some other people appeared and got us out of the ruins. Then we had to wait in the street for transport to take us to the hospital for a check-up.

'While we were waiting I can remember looking up at our houses and seeing the old lady who lived upstairs next door. She was sitting at her kitchen table as if she was having breakfast. She would not move and the services had to go up and carry her down. You could see it all because the whole front of her house had been blown away!

'When I realised that it was a V-2 that had caused the explosion, my thoughts went out to my aunt and her children who lived in the next street (Jackson Street) where the rocket had actually fallen. Thank God they escaped without serious injury – but many of our poor neighbours were killed, and I am glad their names have been put in the Remembrance Book in the hallway of the Memorial Hospital, Woolwich.

'I have another vivid memory of something else that happened just before we were bombed by the rocket. One night a few weeks earlier there was suddenly a great commotion in the street outside our house.

'When I went to the front door, the street was alight with incendiary bombs. I have never seen anything like it – in fact, if there hadn't been a war on you would have said it looked pretty! The wardens were marvellous: they got every one of those bombs out without much damage even though German planes were still flying overhead at the time.'

In a letter to me, Hazel Cooper adds a postscript that her cousin also had a narrow escape from a V-1 which flew over while she was standing outside her house. At first it seemed as if it must fall on her, but instead it dipped and struck the Garrison Church on Woolwich Common – just 300 yards from where she was watching. The building has been left untouched as a memorial to all who died.

'It is very sad to think that Emily went through all that in 1945,' Hazel adds, 'and then last year she died very suddenly at quite an early age. We had gone through so much together.

'I can't put into words just how much I miss her, but I feel that writing my story will be a fitting tribute to a wonderful person. I hope her lovely family will enjoy reading it, too, for they must miss her even more than I do.'

The End of the
Secret Ordeal

Thanks to the RAF bombing raids and the steady Allied advance on Germany, the numbers of V-2s continued to decline during February and March, with the majority of those which were fired being launched after nightfall. But those which struck their targets could still be devastating – as was shown just after 7 a.m. on the morning of 27 March when a V-2 landed on a block of flats in Stepney, killing 134 people and seriously injuring another 49. It was, though, to prove the last major disaster of the rocket war and Hitler's final throw. For although no one knew the fact at the time, that same afternoon, just over nine hours later, the last 'Big Ben' fell on Orpington, Kent. Facts culled jointly from German and British sources were later to reveal that of the 1,403 rockets launched from Holland since the previous September, 517 had fallen in the London Civil Defence Region, 537 elsewhere on land, and 61 offshore, although close enough to be observed. Of the remaining 228 launchings, these had been wild or abortive shots.

Over the next two days, a further half-dozen V-1s were launched against England – the last actually to hit the country exploding harmlessly at Iwade, near Sittingbourne at 10 a.m. on Thursday, 29 March. There was something apt about its failure which symbolised the whole doodlebug campaign – for it had been just nine months earlier that a V-1 had landed beside the same main road at Swanscombe a mere 20 miles to the east…both of them some 40 miles from their intended target of London! The last flying bomb to be seen in English skies did not even reach the coast, but was brought down by ack-ack fire at 12.30 that same day just off the Suffolk coast at Orfordness. Then all fell silent in the air once more…

When a week passed and no further rockets reached the country, Air Chief Marshal Hill realised that his plans had been successful and on 3 April he ordered the end of the bombing raids on all the sites in Holland. By then, all the launching troops had long since returned to Germany. The Doodlebug War was unofficially over – but it was not until Thursday, 27 April that Winston Churchill rose in the Commons to officially announce the fact.

'The V-2 raids have ceased,' he reported quite simply, 'and I think that the people of this country might now have some few moments of rejoicing.'

The statement was typical of Churchill – terse and to the point. This battle might now be over, he cautioned the cheering MPs before sitting down, but the war was still to be won. Pressed by one member if there was any prospect of the attacks being resumed, the PM stood up again and added, 'Well, it is my duty to record facts rather than indulge in prophecy, but I have recorded certain facts with a very considerable air of optimism which I trust will not be brought into mockery by events. It is now time for us to thank the RAF, the Ack-Ack gunners and the Army for all they did.'

The national press was, of course, anxious to lift the veil on the stories of the V-2 attacks which had been kept from print during the previous months. At the forefront of the reports in next morning's papers was Basil Cardew's story, 'The End of the Secret Ordeal', for the *Daily Express.*

Londoners never knew when a new blow would fall upon them during the months of the V-2 rocket attacks. They carried on in their normal lives and they carried on with their war work. Although in one 24-hour period at the height of the offensive 17 rockets fell, people continued their work and production of all kinds proceeded without interruption.

It was during January and February that the attacks reached their peak. The enemy apparently fired the rockets indiscriminately night or day as they were assembled. The Germans were, though, believed to have a preference for loosing off a few early in the morning when the people of England were beginning to stir for the day's work.

In the fight against the V-2, soldiers on leave and civilians powerfully reinforced the Civil Defence services. And on more than one occasion American soldiers helped to save the lives of people buried beneath their homes.

The first rockets fell on 8 September, one in the south of London at Chiswick, the second at Epping. The most devastating of all the V-2s also fell in London, at New Cross, on 25 November, when 168 people were killed. The New Cross disaster stood out in the seven months' ordeal of London – an ordeal that was almost completely secret except for reports by word of mouth to the rest of Britain.

During the time this offensive continued sometimes scores of V-2s arrived in a week. Sometimes the people of London would enjoy peace for two whole days without a bang. Their courage throughout was consummate.

For instance, when a rocket wiped out three of seven blocks of flats in Borough High Street, the people in the remaining four blocks slept in their own beds that same night.

Not a bus was taken off the streets. Theatre and cinema audiences fell off momentarily, but not one manager had to close his doors. Thirty-five hospitals were hit in London and its surroundings, and 45 churches and chapels were completely wrecked or extensively damaged.

But the public houses got it worst. Scores were blasted, dozens were hit – the worst when seven American soldiers were killed in a pub in Duke Street. The men were just about to leave at closing time when the V-2 rocket arrived, blasting parts of Selfridge's store nearby. A taxi passing was blown into the front window and the driver and his passengers were never found.

The second-worst incident occurred on 29 March at Stepney. Workmen who had been toiling throughout the day patching up London from the V-1 bombs had not long got back to their homes at Hughes Mansions and were in bed for the night.

When the rocket streaked to earth at 1,000 miles an hour two blocks of workmen's flats just vanished. A third was also partly wiped out. There were 134 killed that night and 40 lying seriously injured. Many well-known people of Stepney were brought out dead. Among them were Mr and Mrs John Pritchard, both local Aldermen, and Alderman Vellasky, chairman of the Stepney Baths Committee and his wife.

There were whole families killed. Some victims were rescued after many hours being trapped. Mrs John Colberson, for example, could not be freed for six hours. When she was taken away her husband found that he had lost his three daughters. Dogs, including Blood-hounds, were brought in to help find the trapped people. One man heard a brother and sister talking under the debris. They were rescued.

The third-worst V-2 incident at Smithfield on 8 March was a tragedy of a fish queue. The time was 11 a.m. on a bright March morning and the place the junction of Smithfield Market and Farringdon Street. There were large supplies of fish on the stalls. Once again people had queued up to buy the unrationed food.

A woman was stuffing her bag with halibut, the most hard-to-get fish, and her face reflected the achievement. Traffic was at its peak.

Then in an instant before the woman had pocketed her change, the rocket burst, the queue was no more, and the streets were littered with dead and injured. One hundred and fifteen people were killed outright. Hundreds more were taken to hospital and 123 of them were seriously injured.

People who saw the carnage remembered strange incidents. They remembered seeing a man on a milkcart, and after the explosion both the horse and the wagon were there, but the milkman was never seen again. They also told of a woman shopper being blown on to the top of a stall which was collapsed by the blast – or by her weight!

During the whole of the time of the V-2 attacks, *Daily Express* reporters brought back on-the-spot incidents which could not be printed because of the restrictions. One man, for instance, told of the tremendous heroism of girl workers when a rocket hit the Packard factory on the Great West Road in Brentford last month. He said the scene was like a miniature battlefield. The factory was demolished.

Another reporter covered a tea factory which was completely wiped out last month. And although many of the factory girls were injured by flying glass and debris, they refused to go to hospital. They worked until the early hours of the following morning digging for the buried.

Ilford was one of the places on the outskirts of London that had a bad pasting. One V-2 fell behind the stage of the Ilford Hippodrome in January while an audience of 2,000 people were laughing at a pantomime, *Robinson Crusoe*. The explosion burst an overhead tank behind the stage and the orchestra players were drenched with water. But they kept on

209

playing all the same. Three days later the roof of the theatre collapsed.

Nearby Hornchurch has the distinction of being the place where a V-2 fell and failed to explode. The missile landed in March in the garden of a house in Northumberland Avenue, and the earth tremor was sufficient to cause slight damage to four houses. The woman in whose garden it fell was found calmly clearing up the glass. Not until the police told her did she realise what had happened. Then she promptly took her family to safety. So did 250 other people in the district, while bomb disposal experts dealt with the rocket.

A strange incident, still further afield, occurred in an orchard in the centre of the village of Yalding near Maidstone. Peter Curd and Ernest Butler were lopping trees in the orchard. Without any warning a V-2 crashed down and both men were blown out of the trees and temporarily stunned.

'When I came round,' said Curd, 'I found myself lying on the edge of the crater. I heard and saw nothing, but just passed out and then came to at the edge of the hole. My mate also had a lucky escape – although the blast did rip his trousers off!'

It is, of course, impossible to tell the tragic details of all of the V-2 killings that struck at the homes and business life of London. But here are a few more facts that will give an idea of the constant ordeals endured by its citizens.

In March 1945 another serious casualty list resulted when Folkestone Mansions, Deptford got a direct hit, two blocks of flats being demolished. Fifty-two people were killed, 32 more seriously injured. That same month, Whitefield's Tabernacle in Tottenham Court Road was destroyed after catching fire following a direct hit.

'Speaker's Corner', the famous debating ground in Hyde Park which is usually crowded at weekends, was missed by only 40 yards when a rocket fell a few weeks ago. The missile arrived at 9.30 a.m. one Sunday morning when there were few people in the Park and only one passer-by lost his life.

Dalston Public Library was completely destroyed in January, four people who were changing books being killed, two of them children. Five other children passing the library were killed by the blast. In March, 400 boys at Creighton Road Grammar School, Tottenham were on the playing fields when a rocket fell 40 yards away. Two boys died.

There were many casualties when a rocket fell outside a London County Council infectious diseases hospital at Shooter's Hill, Blackheath, in November. A bus caught fire and was gutted and a gas-main burned up many houses.

In January again, a V-2 hit the doctors' quarters at the Royal Hospital, Chelsea, and five people were killed. The famous Pensioners, despite their age and the shock of the blast, joined in the rescue work. One of them, 76-year-old Private John Collins, wearing the North-West Frontier and South Africa medals said, 'I wanted to help, but there it was – you couldn't get near it for helpers.'

Among the churches and chapels destroyed by the rocket weapons were Christchurch, Battersea; Chadworth Chapel, Lambeth; St Paul's Methodist Church, Barking and the Baptist Church, Erith. Those extensively damaged included Trinity Baptist Church, Bexley; The Synagogue, Southgate; St Nicholas' Church, Woolwich; the Presbyterian Assembly House, St Pancras (where many ministers were killed while a meeting was being held); and St John's Church, Beckenham.

The list of hospitals is also extensive and among the 35 hit were: Erith Sanatorium; Banstead Mental Hospital; Herts Sanatorium; Wanstead and Woodford Hospital; the Central Eye Hospital, St Pancras; Royal

211

Alfred Home for Aged Seamen; St Olive's Hospital, Bermondsey; and St Peter's Hospital, Stepney.

Through all these attacks, the Germans never knew where their rockets were falling. No main railway station was hit; no essential building was destroyed that impeded the war effort.

There is no denying that Britain's defence experts had no counter to the 3,000 miles-an-hour robot during its five-minute flight from bases in southern Holland, but by the time the bases had been cut off by the Canadian troops last month we were about to try out counter-measures. Among them was a new secret weapon devised and produced as a result of months of study by Service department chiefs and leading scientists.*

Finally, the average result of all this bombardment – which was occasionally interspersed with a few flying bombs – was that each of the 50-foot, ten-ton missiles killed 2.7 civilians and injured six people. That is the story: London stood the ordeal well. And throughout it all, the secret of the V-2 remained in London and the districts under attack.

*Editor's note: This 'secret weapon' was General Pile's plan for his anti-aircraft gunners to put up a curtain of shell fragments in the radar-predicted path of the approaching rockets to explode them in the air, which, as Air Chief Marshal Sir Roderick Hill mentioned in his article, was made redundant before it could be utilised.

V-3: The German Super-Gun

The lifting of the veil of secrecy following the end of the rocket attacks also enabled the *Daily Telegraph*'s special correspondent, Douglas Williams, who had already reported at length on both the V-1 and V-2 weapons for his paper, to write about the recently discovered V-3 sites in France. He had earlier in the month visited these awesome structures, which, he said, were intended to be used in support of the V-1 and V-2 attacks, and sent the following report from Mimoyecques near Calais. The story takes on an added element of topicality when considered in the light of Iraq's notorious plans to use a super-gun in the Middle East conflict...

Amid desolate chalk hills, six miles from the Channel coast, in an area thickly pitted with yawning bomb holes, I have visited the site of Germany's third secret weapon, the V-3. With this the enemy had planned to fire a continuous barrage of rocket shells from giant cannons into London.

Fortunately for us, the work was detected in its early stages in September 1943. And so successful were the incessant RAF raids that were made on it that construction was seriously delayed. Finally, it had to be abandoned in the summer of 1944 after our Normandy landings.

Had the enemy been able to complete the vast work unimpeded, the installation would have come into operation by the end of last year with devastating effect. The site was designed to accommodate fifty 400-foot-long gun tubes, sunk to a depth of 350 feet below the ground, and protected by a solid 18-foot thick concrete apron.

It is estimated that the monster weapons would have had a combined rate of fire of at least 10 rounds a minute, the shells landing in the heart of London 95 miles away across the Channel. The guns were apparently to have been arranged in twin batteries of 25. They were of a novel design, firing on a fixed line at a high rate of fire with shells of medium calibre, weighing 120 pounds and carrying an explosive charge of 40 pounds.

Being of smooth bore, that is without rifling, the guns would have had life for many thousands of rounds. Fired from a fixed bearing on set elevation, they were presumably designed to maintain a more or less continuous barrage on London day and night.

Apparently it was hoped that with the civilian defence services already fully occupied with the V-bombs and rockets, they would create such havoc as to compel the evacuation of London, with all the administrative complications and damage to British morale that such a step would have involved.

Each section of guns could fire at least five rounds a minute. Once the site had been finished, the thickness of its concrete cover and the depth at which the pieces were embedded would have made it invulnerable to any air attack, no matter how heavy the bombs employed.

The guns would be fired at a high velocity, probably exceeding 5,000 feet per second, at a high elevation. From the direction at which five outlets rising from the low-level workings emerge on the crest of the hill, there is no doubt that London was the only target in mind.

214

Thousands of workers, all slave press-gangs of the Todt Organisation, laboured day and night for nearly a year. The stage of completion, despite the heavy bombing, to which the work had been advanced, pays tribute to the enemy's determination to try at all costs to finish what was obviously a job of the highest order of priority.

No trace has been found of either guns or ammunition. I am informed that some were actually delivered onto the site but they were apparently removed by the Germans when they left, either because they desired to conceal the secret of the new weapon or possibly because they hoped to use them later at another site.

The guns were set in deep inclined shafts, rising from the crescent-shaped chalk hill west of the main Boulogne–Calais road. A standard gauge railway, completed but never used, leads to the site. At the hillside it disappears into a vault-like tunnel of solid concrete of impressive proportions some 700 yards long and 30 feet high by 25 feet broad. An unloading platform giving access to the chambers and galleries opening off the tunnel into the hillside runs its entire length.

Below this main tunnel, at lower levels, are two other smaller tunnels. The entire workings are buried underground, some penetrating to about 350 feet. Superimposed over all, covering an area of several acres, is a slab of concrete up to 18 feet thick in places, pierced with a number of square exits.

At the entrance to the tunnel is another concrete building housing a large electric generator to produce the 4,000 kilowatts of power that the enemy would need to operate this colossal engine of destruction.

In the huge dump of steel girders and unassembled spare parts that were abandoned in the hurry of departure around the workings was found technical machinery indicating the intention to construct a

215

complicated lift system, presumably to handle the ammunition from lower levels.

Today the Mimoyecques site is an abandoned wilderness devastated and churned up by heavy bombs with craters 30 to 50 feet deep. Here and there emerge broken slabs of concrete and portions of huge timbers tossed into the air. But less than a year ago the area was a teeming anthill of action as German engineers pitilessly drove their conscript labour to complete the last refinement in secret weapons which they hoped would finally bring England to her knees.

Mimoyecques was only one of seven so-called heavy sites which the Germans had started to build along the Channel coast, interspersed at strategic localities, in a carefully designed plan to maintain long-range, aggressive action against England with various types of secret V-weapons.

Having a multiplicity of sites, they probably hoped that if one site was temporarily knocked out others would continue in its place. Other installations were situated at Wizernes, Watten, Lottinghem, Stracourt and Sottevaast, and at Martinvasi on the Cherbourg peninsula. They were all primarily aimed at the south coast of England.

Wizernes, in the Calais area, was some form of rocket battery; Watten was chiefly a chemical or ordnance factory; and Lottinghem and Stracourt were flying-bomb sites designed to attack London and southern England.

None had been completed, thanks to our air interference. But little imagination is needed to picture the havoc that seven installations of such tremendous potentialities for destruction could have wrought in thickly populated areas had the enemy been permitted to operate them.

The Wizernes site, about 118 miles from London, was originally spotted by the Air Force in the late summer of 1943. Shortly afterwards air photographs showed a large dome beginning to take shape. The work on this site was finally abandoned in July 1944, about the same time the Germans left Mimoyecques.

The purpose of the Wizernes installation has not yet been clearly established, although it is obvious that the site was designed to fire some form of projectile at England. Experts who have visited the site do not rule out the possibility that it might have been intended to house some other type of secret weapon even more deadly than those we have already encountered.

The most interesting feature of Wizernes is an octagonal chamber over 100 feet in diameter built under the dome, with concrete walls running up to 40 feet thick. Enormous bomb-proof doors had been constructed for it over 50 feet high and about 15 feet wide.

It is believed that through these some form of rocket was to have been fired after the various sections had been brought up from storage rooms below ground and assembled into firing form in the octagon.

Guided Missiles Could Have Won the War

The site at Wizernes that readers of Douglas Williams' article must have thought sounded rather like something from science fiction – but which, in time, would become science *fact* – was indeed intended to be a V-2 launching site. But its discovery, and that of the other sites along the French coast, only served to emphasise the question in many people's minds later that year when the Second World War finally, and thankfully, came to an end: 'If the Germans had been able to bring all their V-weapon plans to fruition could they have won the war?' It is a question that Joseph Warner Angell, an American member of the Crossbow group responsible for countermeasures against the V-weapons and a man who also interviewed several of the surviving German rocket scientists, attempted to answer in an article for the *Atlantic Monthly* in January 1952. The most relevant section is reprinted here.

After 8 September 1944, the Germans fired some 1100 V-2s against England, together with approximately 800 V-1s. Against Continental targets, principally Antwerp, they concentrated a heavy fire of V-1s and V-2s. Belgium suffered far greater damage, proportionately, than did England. In both countries the loss of life and destruction of property was appalling, considering the essentially limited numbers of V-weapons fired by the Germans.

Although only about 2500 V-1s and fewer than 1000 V-2s exploded in England, nearly 10,000 British civilians were killed and some 25,000 were seriously injured. More than 200,000 buildings (principally dwellings) were totally destroyed or damaged beyond repair; 1,339,000 buildings, less seriously damaged, required some type of repair. At least 4,500,000 British civilians were rendered homeless or to some degree inconvenienced. In the second week of September – following the cessation of the major V-1 offensive – a labour force of more than 60,000 – many of them drawn from the armed services – was engaged on repairs to buildings capable of reconstruction.

In Antwerp the damage was even more intense. During the V-weapon attack, which lasted – with only one day's interruption – for 175 days, two thirds of the buildings in the greater Antwerp area were damaged. The dead in Antwerp were nearly 5000, and the number of wounded was in the tens of thousands. The American Consulate General estimated that a fourth of all the buildings in Belgium had been damaged to some extent by the time the last V-weapon was fired, late in March. The cost of replacing Belgian buildings destroyed or damaged was set at approximately $2,000,000,000.

It is impossible to do more than speculate on what Germany might have done with its long-range weapons, notably the V-2, had they been produced in far greater numbers and been committed to combat in the earlier years of the war. Dornberger and von Braun have stated that the V-2 would have been ready for combat as early as 1942 if Hitler had not cancelled Peenemünde's first priority in 1939. The A-10, or transatlantic rocket, could have been operational by 1946, Dornberger suggests, if work on it had continued after the outbreak of war. As to Germany's capacity to manufacture great quantities of the V-2, Willy Messerschmitt, Germany's outstanding aviation authority, is known to have informed Hitler that with an all-out effort at the proper time, German industry could have produced 100,000 V-2s per month.

Though the major responsibility for the German failure to use the V-2 must rest with Hitler, and to some extent with his advisers in the High Command, it cannot be denied that once Hitler decided – in May, 1943 – to use the weapon, there remained unforeseen technical difficulties that had something to do with the failure to use the V-2 before D Day, when it would have been more effective. Von Braun would have it that Hitler's belated decision was doubly wrong, in that he demanded the use of the weapon before it was technically ready.

To what extent the destruction of the original launching sites along the French coast was responsible for the delay in the inauguration of the V-1 offensive is difficult to determine with absolute accuracy. One absolute fact is known about the original launching sites. From the vast network of steel and concrete spread out for hundreds of miles along the coast of France – probably, in its entirety, a construction effort as large as any yet undertaken in peace or war – the Germans launched only *one* missile, a V-1 that misfired. All other V-weapons were fired from mobile sites, developed after the beginning of Allied bombings. In some degree, the continued – and large-scale – construction at the launching sites after the opening of Allied bombing attacks was a purely diversionary operation on the part of the Germans – perhaps Hitler's one good guess in the whole affair. Nevertheless, there is evidence that Hitler, and to some extent the leaders of the Todt Construction Organization, continued building operations at the Large Sites until the very moment they were overrun by Allied ground forces, only because of the German penchant for the colossal. Dornberger explains the long-sustained, grotesquely wasteful, and 'fantastically costly' operations at the

Large Sites – planned to shelter 200,000 personnel and monumental quantities of machinery and supplies – by referring to 'a fatal German weakness – feats for the sake of feats.'

In his last gigantic moments in the underground bunker in Berlin, with the thunder of Russian guns and British and American heavy bombs penetrating the buried recesses of steel and concrete, and with final knowledge that Allied tanks and foot soldiers were closing in from the East and West, it is not impossible that Adolf Hitler remembered certain words he had spoken to a German colonel of artillery two years earlier.

On that day in 1943, ten years after his first visit to the little rocket station at Kummersdorf, Hitler had summoned Dornberger and von Braun to his Personal Headquarters, to tell them that he might use the V-2 against England. When – after seeing the motion pictures that changed his mind, and hearing Dornberger's account of what might yet be done – Hitler emerged from his brooding silence into the storm of words, he furiously rejected Dornberger's modest apology, 'The judgment of its psychological effort, of its usefulness, and of its possible strategic results in this war was not our task. At the beginning of the development we didn't think this rocket should have an all-destroying effect.' Fiercely, Hitler turned to Dornberger and screamed, '*You* didn't intend that, but *I* did!!' And then, in a moment of quiet, Hitler stared searchingly into Dornberger's eyes, and said: 'If only I had had faith in you earlier! In all my life I have owed apologies to two people only – General Field Marshal von Brauchitsch, who repeatedly drew my attention to the importance of [the V-2]...for the future, and yourself. If we had had this rocket in 1939, we would never have had this war. Now and in the future, Europe and the world is too small for war. ... War will become unbearable for the human race.'

Since 1945, when in Europe Hitler and his Germany died and in Asia the first atomic bomb exploded over Hiroshima, the forthcoming era of rocket-atomic warfare has steadily advanced on mankind. No one can know whether Hitler's last words to Dornberger were prophecy or requiem.

Envoi
Rocket to the Moon

It was clear to most people in the spring of 1945 – laymen and scientists alike – that whereas the V-1 had little or no future because it had been proved that it could easily be brought down by guns or fighter planes, the potential of the V-2 had barely begun to be tapped.

Despite the fact that the giant rocket weapon had only come into the war at a very late stage when the Germans had their backs to the wall, it had nevertheless proved itself unstoppable by normal defensive means and apparently limitless in its range. Indeed, even as defeat stared the German technicians in the face, some of them were planning – just as Admiral Ingram had feared – an inter-continental rocket capable of crossing the Atlantic and striking at the very heart of America. They foresaw a future when long-range ballistic missiles carrying nuclear warheads would make the manned bomber completely redundant.

Although, as I mentioned in the Introduction, it was the Americans and Russians who capitalised on the German wizardry that fell into the hands of their advancing forces, it is a fact that it was the British who first put forward plans for trial launchings and testing of the hundreds of abandoned V-2 rockets which were found when the Allied troops entered the vast underground factory where they had been manufactured at Nordhausen in the Harz Mountains on 11 April 1945. To the uncommitted it seemed perhaps only right that the British who had suffered so cruelly under the onslaught of the products of the factory should gain some redress – and consequently some scientific advancement – by taking advantage of these futuristic weapons.

But the Americans had their own ambitions, too, and although a number of their scientists took part in what was, as events transpired, an aptly named exercise, 'Operation Backfire', to assemble and fire a series of V-2s from a site at Cuxhaven on the North Sea coast of Germany, they were already quietly making overtures to both Wernher von Braun and Herman Oberth to continue their work in the United States as part of a programme looking forward to space exploration.

'Operation Backfire' duly took place before invited observers from the Allied nations in October 1945. But already it was evident to the British officials on the spot that the 'top brass' back in Whitehall were now regarding rockets as relics of the war rather than passports to the future. Recommendations from Cuxhaven that the V-2 had tremendous possibilities for development simply backfired on those to whom they were addressed in London – and within weeks some of the German rocket scientists and their hard-won knowledge were on their way to the United States and a mission that, twenty-five years later, would culminate in the giant Saturn V rocket transporting Neil Armstrong to be the first man on the moon. Others were similarly lured to Russia and there, in time, helped launch the Sputnik and the Soviet Union's own mission into space.

Nordhausen – like Peenemünde where the V-1 and V-2 first flew – was kept closed and shuttered by the East Germany authorities and remained so until October 1991. Then, thanks to the reunification, and a realisation of its place in history, proposals for the destruction of the factory in order to allow an extension to gypsum mining already taking place in the mountains, were shelved. Instead, the factory was reopened, and although the rockets and a good deal of technical and scientific equipment had been removed at the end of the war, what remained from when the Russians had sealed the entrance with explosives was found in an almost perfect state of preservation.

Today, this awesome plant with its ten miles of interlaced tunnels where 60,000 prisoners worked day and night to produce Hitler's *Vergeltungswaffe* has been preserved as a memorial not only to the scientific achievements, but more personally to the 20,000 people who were shot, hanged or worked to death in its bowels. It remains a graphic reminder of the extraordinary Flying Bomb War that began with missiles falling on England and launched mankind into space...

Acknowledgements

This book has been many years in the research and writing. I might even say from my own infancy that was spent under the threat of the German V-Weapons and a desire, ever since, to know what actually happened. During this time, sadly, a number of those who helped me are no longer alive, although their spirit lives on in its pages. I would particularly like to record my thanks to the following: Constance Babington Smith, H E Bates, B W Rands, Arthur Geering, A P Herbert, E V Knox, Raymond G Swing, Maurice Ross, Joseph Berry, Roderick Hill, Frederick Pile, Lawrence Fairhall, Frank Gillard, W C Gell, Cecil Smith, Hilary St George Saunders, Hazel Cooper, Basil Cardew, Douglas Williams and especially W O G Lofts, who unearthed a number of the rare contemporary accounts and crucial newspaper stories from the Second World War that are republished herein. Plus the following newspapers and magazines for the use of material from their pages: *The Times, Daily Telegraph, Daily Express, London Gazette, Evening Standard, Evening News, South London Press, West Essex Gazette, Life Magazine, Atlantic Monthly, Collier's Magazine,* and *Punch.* I am also grateful to the staff of the London Library, The British Museum, The British Newspaper Library, The War Museum and the BBC Radio Archives who have likewise assisted me in my attempt to tell the remarkable story of The Flying Bomb War through the words of those who were a part of it.